A *Modern* GUIDE TO
PUBLIC
RELATIONS

AMY ROSENBERG

VERACITY
PORTLAND, ORE.

A Modern Guide to Public Relations: Unveiling the Mystery of PR

A **PR Talk** Resource
Published by Veracity Marketing
4207 SE Woodstock Blvd. #471
Portland, Oregon 97206

Copyright © 2021 Amy Rosenberg

For discounts on bulk purchases or to hire the author to speak visit: **PRtalk.co**

Contributions by Mike Rosenberg, Veracity Marketing

Copyediting by Debra Flickinger

Book cover and interior design by Steve Kuhn, KUHN Design Group

ISBN: 978-1-7365140-0-9 print
        978-1-7365140-1-6 ebook

First Edition

CONTENTS

This book is dedicated to the kids in the front row, let your rebel free,
and to the kids skipping class, you'll end up where you ought to be.

INTRODUCTION

You know *that* kid. They sit in the front row listening with their whole body, poised to participate at all costs. They head off to sports practice, glee club, or student council, insulated by a constant surround of friends. They may or may not be the best on the team, or the smartest in the class, but they show up. Consistently. This kid was made for public relations (PR).

If this is you, you'll go far and it may or may not be easy for you. Your rule-following consistency displays a level of perfection that makes for great PR. You embody the kind of double-checking, detail-orientation that the PR industry classically relies upon.

But if this isn't you, don't leave yet. There is still a place for you here. Your rebel edge may help you in ways you won't be able to recognize. Your flamboyant rule-breaking provides you with a different kind of strength and charisma to leap over those sitting in the front row.

The straight-laced girl happens to live inside of me. After college she thrived within the structure of PR — the editing, the systems, the consistency — of pushing, pushing, pushing for the same thing every day. But this perfect girl always had me glancing over my shoulder. Checking, checking, checking — for what, exactly? Looking for typos, missed meetings, a disaster. None of this ever happened. I thought this was the mark of a great PR person.

Yet, I was so hard on myself, even causing the pattern of my breathing to change as I opened up my own PR firm. I wondered what my new clients thought of me: Was I doing enough? Was I getting enough? Was I enough?

I made a drastic change in my life. Reaching far into my past for the rebel I once was, I welcomed her back. The perfect girl recognized the rebel immediately, telling her she could stay, but only on her terms. The rebel leaned in for once, eager to be part of it all.

Today the rebel mostly abides by the perfect girl's rules. But out in the world, away from the protection of the computer screen, the rebel inserts herself. She's the one who interrupts when spoken over and holds the audacity to say no.

The perfect girl helps me show up everyday, not only for others, but also for myself. But the rebel holds her hand, telling her that mistakes are made to be made and that everything is going to be OK.

It is the rebel that brings me to fearlessness, steadying my breath along the way.

For more on classic PR perfectionism, listen to
PR Talk podcast episode #54 on **PRtalk.co**

"I want to work with people," I said.

"Have you ever worked with the media?," he asked. I told him about my experience working as the director at a summer camp for military kids in Italy. One time I'd played secretary, helping the military TV station put together a story featuring our camp.

"So you 'set it up'," he clarified.

"Well, yes I did," I said, going into the details of the secretarial work I'd performed.

Recognizing this "set it up" to be important, I expanded upon it for him. I didn't know then what I know now. The intuition required to pick up on important nuances and create more out of them, like this "set it up" instance, meant I was destined for PR.

No one told me that PR is about so much more than working with people. It can be the introvert's writing outlet, the analyst's numbers game, the psychologist's counseling session, the salesman's cold call, or the social butterfly's party.

I got that summer internship and the man sitting across from me ended up being my first public relations guide. I quickly found myself spending more time on the actual work of PR than the tasks I'd been assigned as an intern. At one point I asked if I had to do the dishes. They laughed at my gumption, missing the point. It wasn't about the dishes. It was the PR work being left undone that I couldn't take.

I never did grow into my humility while at that first job, but they saw something in me as I worked stuffing press kits well past my 3 p.m. intern stopping time. After a month I was promoted from intern to half receptionist, half entry-level PR. The split role caused interruption from the cerebral work of PR. It didn't last long because they valued my PR work.

Co-owned by a mother and son duo, there were two bosses. The mother was a small, blonde, dynamite of a personality who was brave enough to swim through the murky waters of professionalism back when it wasn't common for women to do so. She wasn't sure that I had "it."

Her son, the man who had interviewed me, recognized the "it" in me. With his mother's foot halfway out the door toward retirement, he was around more. He taught me half of what I know about PR and for that I am forever grateful.

> For more on my background, listen to PR Talk
> podcast episode #50 on **PRtalk.co**

CHAPTER ONE

PR 101

PR stands for: Public Relations. So, in a general sense it's about relating to the public. There are many ways to do this, depending on the communication tools you have at your disposal and how your audience consumes information.

Suppose you're a nun at a nunnery in a small Italian town on the west coast of the Tyrrhenian Sea. And it's your job to get the nuns the information they need to complete service work, informing them of the outside community's needs and relaying news of what's going on inside the nunnery to the public. You might not have this title, but you're essentially acting as the nunnery's PR director!

Now let's suppose you're working at an IT startup in Silicon Valley. It's new and small so you don't quite know what your role is yet, but you've become tasked with relating the news of what's going on inside the organization to the outside world. And sometimes vice versa. Congratulations! You're also acting as the PR director!

The *way* each person communicates, *what* they communicate, and to *whom* might be starkly different for each role. But the two jobs are quite similar. PR serves as a conduit between where you are (inside the walls of your organization) to where you want to be (in front of certain audiences without necessarily leaving). You're getting a message, or multiple messages, from inside your organization to specific audiences. At times the role can be fluid — alternating from communicating to the outside to speaking directly to those inside your organization or surrounding stakeholders.

A mountain of different types of PR exist, from internal relations and public affairs to community relations and investor relations. But this is a guide to classic media relations, which can be explained as the way in which an organization relates to the media. Media relations is likely the most well-known type of PR, therefore it's typically simply generalized as "PR."

HOW PR IS DIFFERENT

It used to drive me bonkers when people would call everything related to marketing: PR. It was confusing! I would worry when they'd lump PR into the advertising category, because I wanted everyone to know I wasn't responsible for the outrageous ad buy or the ugly logo design. But even more than that, it was a personal protection thing. I had enough on my plate to worry about; thank you very much. I didn't want the groups I worked with to assume I would handle everything that potentially falls under the marketing umbrella.

However, over the years I've come to realize that some people use PR as a phrase that could mean just about anything. Today, I view such broad generalization as a compliment. PR is relevant to all marketing aspects, along with many of the most crucial parts of an organization's operation. How cool is that?

Still...it will help you do your job better if you can describe the difference between PR and advertising. Let me arm you with the two primary differences between placing an advertisement and the golden standard of getting media to cover you.

PR is FREE

Kind of. Sure there is the point that nothing in life is free. The PR firm or in-house marketing team needs to be paid, or if you as the head of your organization are also saddled with PR tasks, there is your time, which could never pass as free.

But, you don't actually have to pay the media outlet when you get *earned* media coverage — you *earned* it after all! Earned media is a common term for PR in relation to advertising, whereas advertising has been dubbed *paid* media. Certainly in PR there is a surcharge for the time and expertise required from whomever is seeking coverage. But after the work is done, it can be a coverage "free-for-all;" sometimes resulting in return trips to the buffet, all for the price of one.

Plus, even if you are paying a PR firm what may seem like excessive fees, in most cases those fees will cost less than what you'd pay to place an advertising buy. Just think, after paying the outlets where your ads will be placed, then what? Someone still has to be paid to write and design the ads. Also, there's a lot of pressure wrapped up in creating just the right thing when you're paying for placement, which is why many organizations also end up paying designers and writers.

PR is Credible

According to Cision's 2018 State of the Media Report[*], 56 percent of journalists say fake news accusations are causing audiences to become more skeptical. While that means it is even harder for brands to ensure credibility, it presents an opportunity for PR to assert itself through carefully researched, well-written content in order to build credibility with audiences.

Although you can find varying opinions about the greater credibility of earned media versus paid advertising, in a 2019 study conducted by the

---

* cision.com/us/2018/05/2018-state-of-media-infographic/

Institute for PR[*], the greatest percentage of participants stated they found the earned media story, including blogs written by independent sources, to be the most credible. The study goes on to state, "People believe that advertisements are a necessary component of the promotional mix to build awareness. People recognize that the information contained in an advertisement may be somewhat biased because the company paid for it, yet they temper that understanding with a critical review of the information and a desire to seek *outside verification* of the claims made. People recognize that companies will face legal consequences if they don't tell the truth."

Look at it this way: Most people know that anyone with some cash and resources can place an advertisement. If I see an advertisement for a nutritional supplement I've never heard of before, I'll likely skim past it, not even questioning whether or not I'd be comfortable ingesting the ingredients found within it. But when a journalist references a scientific study pointing to the health benefits for said supplement, I may find myself purchasing the supplement the next time I come across their advertisement.

> For more on what PR is and how it is different, listen to PR Talk podcast episode #62 on **PRtalk.co**

WHAT KIND OF PR PERSON ARE YOU GOING TO BE?

Who you choose to be in PR may shift over the course of your career. Your role within PR may change, the industry you're representing may change, your entire job description may change — pulling you away

---

* instituteforpr.org/understanding-how-changing-media-sources-in-the-promotional-mix-inform-credibility-and-consumer-action/

from the everyday work of PR. No matter what you do, however, your PR training will always be with you.

With such training, here are the roles you can play in PR, but remember that your PR mindset can take you far and into many other exciting careers.

The Publicist (Fancy Stereotypes)

This is the quintessential, or *stereotypical*, PR person. They organize red carpets (or make sure their clients are on them) often attending impressive events and being in the spotlight in the PR way. That means they are off to the side, behind the client who is the star. Always. It is their job to ensure it. Publicists get things placed in the media, creating buzz, most often of the consumer variety. They don't always have to work in the red carpet arena, but they spend their days building the most amount of public attention possible.

The B2B'er (Company Communications)

This person promotes businesses among other businesses, most often through trade and vertical press. They are doing very business-y things and acting very business like. Their work is much more predictable, 9-to-5 like, than the publicist's, but it still can get quite busy depending on how hard they push. They may use trade shows, which can have their own amount of chaos to them, as a way to meet press and influencers within the industries they are trying to influence themselves.

The Numbers-Pusher (Investor Relations)

This hallmark investor relations position is locked into the financial world. The numbers-pusher works for public companies or financial institutions that rely on what analysts say about them. Essentially, *analysts* are the numbers-pusher's outside spokesperson — their good or bad opinions possibly ending up in the news — ultimately influencing the financial markets, which could mean more (or less) money in share-holders' pockets.

The Do-Gooder (Community Relations)

Community relations is the practice of aligning your organization's interests with a community group, cause or charity. While community relations work can be leveraged through earned media, external praise may not be the deciding factor for organizations considering community involvement. Some organizations really do want to connect with their communities on an intimate level for no other reason than to build goodwill, strengthening relationships through activities that sometimes pair with monetary donations.

The Inside-Agent (Internal Relations)

Some organizations view their workforce as not only their most valuable asset, but also their megaphone. Employees can be an organization's best evangelists. Some can be major money-makers for organizations or the only income-generating source. The inside-agent is not in charge of HR, which handles paperwork, benefits, vacations, etc. They instead communicate directly to the employees with distinct purposes like building goodwill, softening changes, or evangelizing employees through tools like internal newsletters and podcasts or private Facebook groups.

> For more on Internal Communications, listen to PR Talk podcast episode #56 with Chuck Gose on **PRtalk.co**

The Fire-Stopper (Crisis Response)

The fire-stopper image may be one of high-powered suits swooping in and out of problems mid-disaster to assemble triage. Yet, ideally all PR people work ahead of the crisis, preventing it from occurring in the first place through careful planning and immaculate team integration, while choosing to work with organizations that are in the practice of doing the right thing. But, sometimes someone gets caught with their pants down and it's the fire-stopper's job to fix it. Fire-stoppers hold the kind of instinct that comes from years of experience. They've spent their careers trying new things by being open to failure, viewing all mistakes as opportunities to learn, and carefully emulating, or sometimes most importantly not emulating, those that have gone before them.

The Glad-Hander (Public Affairs)

This person is a governmental baller. While they don't have to actually work in the government, their job is to affect public policy through communications that influence those who typically should not be influenced — the government — using their savvy to either bring about change or to stop it from occurring. Besides connecting with lobbyists and orchestrating glad-handing, public affairs staff can work to publish key stories seen by members of the government, or the voting public, to influence rules and regulations affecting all kinds of things.

The Mouth-Piece (Public Information Officer (PIO))

Pictured with a megaphone in their hand, the PIO is the spokesperson for government and NGO organizations like the city, fire department or a public utility. They are the first responders on the scene when something goes wrong and have to answer to the public through the press and in social media. Since they are essentially on-call at all hours of the day or night, ideally there would be a few of them working within an organization to rotate availability. But speaking with the press isn't all they do, they also must handle many, if not all, of the roles listed in this section.

For more on PIOs, listen to PR Talk podcast episode #32 with Dave Thompson, former PIO of Oregon's Department of Transportation, on **PRtalk.co**

The Strategist (Account/PR Director)

Every PR campaign should be rooted in strategy. There is a difference between reactively opening a TikTok account just because someone tells you to and first asking why. Audiences, goals, and the reasoning behind every action should be mapped out before launching head-first into any PR campaign. But it's the strategist's entire job to always be planning, thinking, calculating.

———

This list is only a beginning. I could go on and on with link builder/ SEO PR, social/influencer PR, researchers and many more. Essentially, most PR professionals are hybrids of a few, or all, of these fluid roles.

> For more on PR roles and mindset, listen to
> PR Talk podcast episode #60 on **PRtalk.co**

Since I'm a do'er this book is about doing. Of course we'll touch on strategy, but sometimes the best reasoning stems from the discovery of action.

While each of these roles sound very different, there is much overlap. Executives may find themselves combining pieces of each of these jobs into an entire role. But most importantly, working in any PR capacity will build a successful PR mindset. The PR mindset can be summed up with three points:

- Maximization — turning one story into 20

- Details — placing equal weight on the largest and smallest of details

- Tenacity — following up relentlessly, not just with the media, but also with clients or internally to get what needs doing done

These highly sought after skills are invaluable in any professional setting, whichever way your PR career may take you.

CHAPTER TWO

FORGET YOUR STORY

As you think about starting press outreach, it can be normal to feel apprehensive about the story you want to tell. You may think you must uncover your organization's perfect "story" before you can start outreach.

Don't let the quest for the perfect story create a block that paralyzes you. Remember, attempting to perfect your story can be an overwhelming place to start, even for practiced story-tellers. It's not that there isn't a story to be uncovered, but it can take time to understand an organization's identity and how to position it best.

Avoid letting perfection riddled insecurity stop you from getting a start on your PR. Hopefully the sections ahead will provide you with enough ideas, because it would be a shame to let finding the perfect story stand in the way.

I say, forget your story! You have to start somewhere, so start with the news.

GENERATING NEWS IDEAS

In deciding what is "*news*," ask yourself what's *new* in your organization. Write down a list of everything that comes to mind in the section below or grab a piece of scratch paper. You're just warming up with a brainstorm. There are no wrong answers. As your juices start flowing you might stumble upon a winning idea.

A list of what the media typically covers follows this section, but DON'T SKIP AHEAD TO THAT PART. Lists can sometimes pigeon-hole our minds. I want you to come up with your own ideas.

WHAT'S NEW?

Armed with your ideas, you might be unsure as to whether or not they are any good. It doesn't really matter if they are good as long as just one media member covers it (in a positive light).

If you want to know if the news would cover something, pay attention to the news. Any news will do, but it's even better if it's related to your specific industry, cause, location or audience. Make reading, listening and watching the news a habit. I repeat. Make it a habit.

If you're too busy to follow the news, why should a reporter make time to read your email? Warm up your PR mind with the news of the day in the morning. You can listen to Brittney, J Lo and Snoop later, as you end your day.

> For more on why your story doesn't matter and press release topics, listen to PR Talk podcast episode #64 on **PRtalk.co**

LIST OF NEWS IDEAS

What Press Release Types the Media Will Actually Cover

Now that you have your ideas, here's a cheat sheet of the press release types a business section, local community paper/section, or industry press might cover. Do not read this list until you've followed the instructions in the first paragraph of this section.

We're not talking about front page stories (it depends on the publication) or television news segments (it depends on how you frame the story and where you are), but we are now getting into the *what* of PR. What to communicate if sending a press release. Most bigger stories stem from either these, or other, ideas and are typically not generated through press releases.

In general, you are attempting to do something within the community or industry where you want coverage and then the following news ideas can stem from there:

- Executive joins a board/committee

- Donation to a cause

- New location opening

- New service or product creation

- Notable new person hired

- Construction of a new development/building

- Launch/results of a new scientific study

- Community involvement/volunteering

- Events, photo ops and press conferences

- Recap what you did (events, fundraising and company results, such as growth)*

Whether from your ideas and/or the list above, you have the beginning of a PR plan and you didn't even have to talk about your "story." Prioritize the ideas as you prepare to build your plan.

I know you want to know the *way* to announce your top ideas. You might be excited about one of the ideas and think it is press release time. Some of you may have already fired up your computer, fingertips at the ready to shoot off your first official press release. Gosh, the press release sure lends an important tone to a situation, doesn't it? Let me stop you right there. While the list above may indicate the primary instances where a press release would be used, *if a press release is even necessary,* we are still at the very beginning of becoming PR-savvy.

While these topics can call for press releases, a release isn't the only way

---

* More about recap press releases on PRtalk.co

to promote all these ideas. In fact, these ideas often need more than just a press release for maximum exposure.

However, when the time comes for a press release, there are some general instructions in the following sections or follow the sample press release templates that relate to some of the ideas listed above, with more explanation about recap press releases, at PRtalk.co.

For more on when to use a press release, listen to
PR Talk podcast episode #67 on **PRtalk.co**

CHAPTER THREE

YOUR PR TOOLBOX

You might think that the most important PR tool is your mind, but it's not. It's your instinct. Learn how to listen to your gut and adjust, because in PR the world is fluid. You'll be working with people you wouldn't naturally jive with, creating messages for different points-of-view, and pivoting direction amid an ever-changing digital news world — often all in one day. But for now, we're still getting comfortable with the basics.

Here are the few tools you'll incorporate into your toolbox:

- The Press Release

Probably more important tools:

- The Press Pitch
- Photos and Videos
- Media Databases/Media Lists
- Blog Posts (the new press release)

- Press Kits and Virtual Press Rooms
- Media Drops
- Snail Mail
- The Telephone

THE PRESS RELEASE

Think of the words "for immediate release" — the hallmark beginning lines of a press release — as an invitation for the press to use some or all of the words that follow within the press release. It's understood that the press can use the words verbatim or they can use a portion of the words or even switch the structure of the content around.

How often the press actually accepts this invitation to use the words verbatim in a press release depends. While not as much of a sure-thing as it used to be, it still happens if you're writing for a very specific press audience. Declining journalism budgets mean there aren't enough reporters to properly cover all the stories at their disposal. For the most part this works to our disadvantage, but you could also hit the jackpot because of it. The press picks up your release verbatim because they don't have the staff to put their own stamp on the story. Your client or boss is paying for your contribution to a newsroom but gaining much more in return.

Today, it's unlikely that verbatim pick-up will occur with the big players like the *New York Times.* But I believe that a long, long, long time ago — like before women were even allowed in board rooms — it did work this way with many publications. The PR industry is hooked into that memory, trying to recreate the success of the first press releases of the past.

The cold, stark reality is that most press releases don't run. Many of us know this, but we still use the release to appease our clients or bosses. Some of us still actually believe the release will entice the media to go deeper into the story while putting their own journalistic spin on it. If you have a rich story that you know a journalist would love to sink their teeth into, and you're thinking the press release will get them to do that, you might consider joining us in the present day.

In that case, you're probably wondering, what the point of the press release even is. There needs to be a point to everything we do. We don't spend grueling hours sweating it out for the love of exercise. The same goes for the press release. The biggest mistake a PR person can make is believing their work is over after the press release is written. Most of the clients, bosses and general public are under this illusion. We need to educate them that **the point of the press release is to get press coverage.**

So, the most important work for the press release begins before you actually set down the words "for immediate release." It lies within the research and development phase.

Then you've got to get the darn thing to run. Getting actual publication requires in-depth press research, follow up and pitching.

If your press release doesn't fall within the prerequisite news categories listed in Chapter 2, opt for better ways of communicating, such as:

- Short email pitches
- Phone calls (sometimes followed by email pitches)
- Coffee dates, lunches and happy hours (with or without your client or boss)
- Blog posts
- Social media campaigns geared toward your key media audience
- Op-Eds and bylined articles

When a Press Release is Better than a Press Pitch

Since so many instances call for pitches over press releases, you're probably wondering why you'd ever need to fumble through writing a press release. Technically, you never have to write a press release again. However, the "release" brings more structure to smaller stories, sometimes resulting in more ink. Since releases remind us to quote key players and add details like physical addresses, we end up turning what might only be published as a two sentence news brief into a small two paragraph story (with pictures of course!).

Here is an example. Your company hired some schmuck out of Ohio. This new guy, with little experience, came into the office looking like Milton from "Office Space." A stuttering, babbling excuse for a vice president of marketing. OK, maybe you're a little miffed because you thought your two years of experience would win you the promotion. Do not fret. Your new PR skills will win them over yet. It's only a matter of time.

Back to Milton. Other than listing a couple of non-highlights from his lackluster LinkedIn profile, there really isn't much else to say about him. But if you start with the new hire press release template found on PRtalk. co, you'll remember to throw some extra lines together, quoting his manager about why they chose Milton [over you!]. You could then incorporate a quote from Milton about why he's excited to join your organization. You'll probably have to make this quote up for Milton because I'm assuming he couldn't string a sentence together if his life depended on it.

Now you have a little more for the press to copy from your press release and paste into their publication or website. This process works for all the press release examples in Chapter 2 if you have time.

> Get press release approval from your boss or client before distribution. Get quote approval from all quoted parties. Save all approvals.

How to Write Press Releases

Believe it or not, writing press releases can be tricky. That's why most people hate them! They can be extremely difficult for long-form writers to master because of their simplicity. Clean and compact writing packed with key information requires skill.

Most press releases should be about a page, while press pitches can be just a paragraph or two. You're probably wondering how a press release could be a full page, while the desired length for a press pitch is less than a few paragraphs. First of all, you never send press releases to just anyone for the sake of sending press releases. You've meticulously researched your media list and are only reaching out to contacts you know will be interested in your news. Maybe you've been operating this way for a while, building up credibility as someone who doesn't mess around, so your releases are taken seriously.

Regardless, the media doesn't really read the full press release even if they intend to use it. Instead they are skimming the email subject line/ headline to see if it remotely relates to what they cover. If it passes muster, they are in working mode with your release, dissecting it to fit with their publication's format. So make sure your press release is written in a way that will be easy for them to use. Anything riddled with typos could overwhelm the most patient of reporters who are happy to delete your press release.

One of your main roles in PR is to help the media with their jobs. Imagine if thousands of pitches flooded your in-box each hour. Your phone ringing off the hook with calls from PR people — college-educated telemarketers in disguise — a couple hundred times a day. You have multiple deadlines hanging over your head, a harsh editor to contend with, and a handful of fresh-faced college kids jockeying for the job that's only paid you $45,000 for the last two years. Oh, and the ad reps are having a heck of a time pulling in the revenue to keep your department afloat.

"What was it you wanted again?," the harried reporter poses in response to your indulgent phone call.

AP Style

In an effort to help the media with their jobs, your press release needs to be perfect in the most boring sense of the word. Associated Press ("AP") style is the go-to journalism writing rulebook. Not all bloggers abide by these standards, but some of them used to be journalists so they might. AP style isn't really that big of a deal, but it presents a consistent standard and cleaner, clearer way to write.

Some of the rules are great for all writers to follow, but most are just weird habits that we still blindly follow today. I've noticed journalists veering away from more stringent rules, if their editors and publishers let them. Therefore, my own standards have softened. I'm constantly surprised how after 20 years of fretting about AP style I can still forget the rules. While many of the rules don't matter, some will scream your beginner status if broken.

Let's not embarrass ourselves, abide by these main AP guidelines:

One Space Between Sentences

I don't know if this is technically an AP style rule but it's the top on my list....shows ya how important the AP style rules are. You must not write with two spaces between sentences. It is ugly, clunky and makes you look like an idiot. I don't care what they told you in high school. Just don't do it. We're adults now who write with one space between sentences. Period.

State Abbreviations

A classic AP style that most press releases still follow is state abbreviations. We don't abbreviate the states in the way the post office does. For instance, California is not CA, it is Calif. While Oregon is not OR, it is Ore. Why? It might make it easier to discern two states from each other if they both start with the same letter. But I have a sneaking suspicion that it started as yet another way for the press to exert their special status.

Other Miscellanea

There are specific ways to write physical addresses, titles, dates, days, dimensions, monetary units, months, numbers, time, etc. The AP stylebook basically tells you when you'd spell these things out or use abbreviations.

———

This will become second nature, but the most important point to remember is that none of this really matters. If AP style is getting in the way of actually sending press releases out, please just send your press release out. People are a lot more forgiving today and it's PR people who dangle AP style over everyone's heads to intimidate everyone into thinking they can't take part. If your writing is clean and clear and your media list solid, you're a lot farther ahead than the PR purists who whip out the AP stylebook.

If you find yourself in the middle of a press release unsure about the correct way to proceed, just Google it! Millions of people are online waiting to solve your problems. Or buy the latest version of the book at APStylebook.com. It's constantly updated.

PRESS RELEASE FORMATS

There are three types of press releases used in specific scenarios:

1. Media Advisories/Calendar Listings

2. Fact Sheets

3. General Press Releases

I consider media advisories, fact sheets and calendar listings to be similar because they aren't in normal paragraph format, therefore they are distinctly different from general press releases. However, some people can get a little prickly about semantics and we wouldn't want to cause a ruckus. Here are the differences and when you'd use each.

Media Advisories/Calendar Listings

With events, press conferences — or anything you are inviting people to — it's best to follow a "Who, What, Where, When, Why" format, listed underneath a headline and possibly subhead. This is technically called a media advisory or a calendar listing. I often switch the order of the "Who, What, Where, When, Why" categories depending on which messages I want to convey first. **The farther the eye travels down the page, the more readers are lost.**

Fact Sheets

Fact sheets are used when listing the facts, offering a seamless way to present key information at-a-glance. After the headline, and possibly subhead, each subject is detailed after special headers that introduce each topic. Fact sheets can be used for organizations, causes, products, services, events, whatever. A large company could rely on multiple fact sheets: one outlining its executive team, another for its board of directors, and more for various products, services, locations, historical information, ad infinitum.

These don't necessarily have to follow the standard "Who, What, When, Where, Why" format. They could, although you might want to remove the "When" and the "Where" if you aren't inviting anyone anywhere. Or not, because "When" the company was founded and "Where" it is located also come to mind. You can get creative with fact sheets — incorporating graphs in the history sheet, headshots in the executive sheet, and infographics in the services sheet.

Since you have a lot of leeway with fact sheets, I won't detail their general format.

General Press Releases

These releases are in "normal" paragraph format, but you can get a little funky with them. For instance including bullet points in the middle of the release to list statistics, percentages, or important points. Or including a highlighted "Where and When" section for smaller events that are part of a larger announcement.

But if you aren't down with the funk, a basic old-school press release format follows an example of a media advisory/calendar listing template.

MEDIA ADVISORY / CALENDAR
LISTING TEMPLATE

Headline: Using an Action Statement, Clearly State the News

Subhead: secondary header if
necessary, which it isn't always

FOR IMMEDIATE RELEASE — Dateline (city, state of where your news is happening, date of distribution) — Followed by an introductory paragraph if you want. You might not even want the date in the dateline if you are announcing multiple dates in a calendar listing. I sometimes find that confusing. You might just want to focus on the date(s) you are announcing.

WHAT: Concisely state what is happening. Try to hook media by painting a visual of what they'll see (very important for TV), or capturing the sounds they'll hear (very important for radio), and/or tying in what is *newsworthy* or *timely* about what you're sending them.

WHEN: Include the date the event is occurring. Duh. An editor told me event listings failing to include the date will sometimes grace his in-box. Do not be this PR person.

WHERE: Think beyond only the location. Include special instructions for where media can park, clearance for live truck towers, etc.

WHY: If you are incorporating a charitable cause, include it here (as well as in the header or "What" sections, because remember people might not read this far down), along with any *newsworthy* or *timely* bits you've surely included up top too.

WHO: This can be a nice place to list sponsors who are paying to be in your press release. However, if they are presenting sponsors you must include them once in the title of the event. Or if you want to give more information about who is organizing your event or more about how the event's beneficiary was founded, by all means, do it here. This section can also include any prominent people expected to attend.

Boilerplate: you don't always have to use it
in media advisories but it is a tiny little annoying
PR thing and we will get to what it is soon.

# # #

Insert your contact information here at the end. Include your name, organization, phone number where they can reach you both before event day and at the event, which any respectable PR person would consider to be a cell phone that's with you at all times.

Get approval, including quote approval from all quoted parties, before distribution. Save all approvals.

GENERAL PRESS RELEASE TEMPLATE

Headline: Using an Action Statement, Clearly State the News

*Subhead: secondary header
if necessary, which it isn't always*

FOR IMMEDIATE RELEASE — **Dateline** — Introduce your news in the first paragraph. It might help to also think of this in a *who, what, where, when, why* format — paragraph style. *What* is going on? *Who* is involved? *Where* (area or population) does this effect? *When* did or will this happen? Include the timely piece, even if you don't have a *when,* because you always need somewhat of *when*-type information.

Possibly the *why* or even more specific *who, what, where, when* details would fall here, in the second paragraph.

"Include your first quote either here, or in the second paragraph, if it makes more sense to encapsulate your details in a quote," said first and last name, title, organization. "Do not bury your quote too far down and follow this exact format. Never bury a first quote inside the words of a bulky paragraph, make it stand out as its own paragraph." [NOTE: It is okay to "make up" a quote and ask for approval/modification.]

More specifics here, if necessary. Further explain your *why* with statistics or supporting research, although quotes can detail *why's* without hard numbers or research. I personally don't like a press release that simply lists quote after quote. It could be done in a pinch or when working with multiple parties. But know that listing quote after quote is lazy. If you need to quote several people, it may warrant creating multiple customized releases for more specific audiences.

"Here is where your second quote, if you need one, can go. Either further explain by quoting the same person, in which case end the quote with just their last name because you don't need to re-introduce their organization and title," said last name. "Or introduce another person, such as a sponsor. It may be important that the sponsor is included in the actual news that results from this press release, in which case, quote them first."

Either end here with the boiler plate or add a few more supporting lines to your *who, what, where, when, why.* You can of course have more than two quotes in a press release, but this probably means you're trying to make multiple people happy. Remember that the farther down the eye travels, the less likely the lower content will get included in the actual news. Knowing this can give you some semblance of control in an uncontrollable field and is the kind of strategic thinking that PR is about. It's not about putting down fancy words in a pretty press release, it's about writing the strongest content you can to increase the likelihood of publication.

We end with the classic boilerplate. "Boilerplate" means that it is the same in every document. Many clients or bosses think this is very important. But because it's at the bottom of the press release we know that it's not. We humor them anyways. This shouldn't be much longer than five sentences explaining what your organization is about, who (including geographical areas) it serves, unique or specific products or services, general organizational website (with link) and social media handles.

#

Get approval, including quote approval from all quoted parties, before distribution. Save all approvals.

WHAT ALL PRESS RELEASES HAVE

The Boring Details

Besides being *newsworthy* and *timely*, there are elements to a press release that are consistent with each one you write. Most of these elements don't actually make your press release better, increasing the likelihood it will actually generate news, but they are in the press release probably as a form of habit. Here is what they are:

FOR IMMEDIATE RELEASE

Not only does this line classify the document as a press release, it means that the information in the document can be used, verbatim or not, immediately.

If you want to put an "embargo" (delayed release time) on your news, you'd indicate this by phrasing the line like this: FOR EMBARGOED RELEASE on [insert date]. You would embargo news when you want to give the media a heads up about something, but you don't want that news to go public until a particular time.

Headline

This is the most important part of your release but not as important as the email subject line. Every press release needs a headline.

Dateline

This should list the city and state where your news is happening, followed by the date you send your press release out. However, there may be occasions when you do not include the date in the dateline. Some releases are longstanding and can be applied to any point in time — so putting a date on it could increase the likelihood that it's trashed if the media thinks it's old. The same goes for event calendar listings, you may forgo the date because it could confuse with other dates in the body of the release.

You can also customize the location of the dateline depending on where you are sending the release from or what area you're distributing the news to.

The dateline should look something like below, following the same capitalization and bolding style, to ensure consistency.

CITY, Sta. – insert date

Go right into your news here.

Website Links

Hyperlink to your organization's website in the press release. In fact, you might consider establishing a website if you don't already have one before commencing PR.

You can also hyperlink to external websites to cite references or provide a place where additional information about any partners or other organizations can be found.

Boilerplate

The end of every release will have a paragraph that's the same for that particular organization or cause. It can be updated periodically or when something changes. The press release format example (previously explained) details boilerplates in greater detail. Because I know you're skipping ahead.

#

The three-hash-mark symbol denotes that the press release has ended, a rule of thumb that is universally understood by the media. The three hash-marks, or alternatively, the -30- symbol are said to have originated during the Civil War as a telegraphic shorthand.

Although it can be mystifying why such old formats ensue, in all honesty, details like these bring a comforting, nostalgic air to what might be a dying art form. I've always been fond of admiring my handiwork on the page, wanting it to look good. My headline must be nicely centered and I value the balance the # # # symbol brings to the design. Plus, the best way to get over writer's block is to just get started. Beginning with the words FOR IMMEDIATE RELEASE is sometimes all that's needed to get up and going.

WHAT ALL PRESS RELEASES *SHOULD* HAVE

To Increase Odds It Will Actually Run

More important than the little press release details, such as the boiler plate and AP style, is what the press release is actually saying. The meat of it. Press releases, or any media communication in which you are trying to land coverage, should have both of these elements: *newsworthiness* and *timeliness.*

Newsworthiness

You can look at newsworthiness a couple of ways. Being newsworthy might hook into some news that is already happening, or perhaps even better, you could actually create your own news.

Be careful with hooking into news that is already happening because it could be viewed as crass, or taking advantage of a situation, depending on the news.

While creating your own news may seem more intimidating, it is actually somewhat the beginning point of all PR campaigns. PR campaigns do not begin with the act of writing the press release. Rather, the press release, or any material or ensuing coverage, is the result of what you've done to plan ahead. The press release creation should be the easy part, if you have done your due diligence to either dig up the "news" or create the news to be detailed in your press release.

Timeliness

You've heard the phrase: Timing is everything. This couldn't be more true in PR. There are many ways to consider timing in PR, from when to distribute a press release and how it outlines timely angles, to the key moment for following up, which could be locked down to the minute.

Act fast if you are going to play the timing game. If you attempt to hook into news that is occurring too late, there is no point as you'll have lost your moment. You'll also have to think beyond the press release and ensure your interviews are ready to go at a moment's notice after contacting the press because if not, the press will just find a different source and you'll have lost your opportunity.

But, if you aren't trying to hook into the changing tide of current news, you'll need to have a crystal ball to hook into what you know will be on the horizon. Holidays, seasons and seasonal themes — such as spring cleaning and back-to-school — are great ways to start thinking strategically. Other big happenings we already know about, such as political elections or huge consumer events, are also excellent opportunities to build your story around.

Timeliness means not only considering *when* to distribute but also *how* to bring the theme front and center into your press release. Editorial calendars can provide us with a great cheat-sheet on timely themes as they outline what the press will be working on when — truly arming you with a crystal ball.

Don't worry, I've got you. You'll learn all about these additional ways to be a badass PR pro in the following chapters.

PROBABLY MORE IMPORTANT TOOLS

THE PRESS PITCH

Think of the press pitch like a proposal of sorts. These persuasively written emails are meant to convince the press to pick up what you're throwing down. You are asking the press to do something for you, such as:

- Cover a story idea that could incorporate your organization, like sharing opinions on industry trends, current events or breaking news.

- Include your organization in a story you know the press is probably already working on, with your client becoming the "source." You can guess what they are covering through researching their publication, editorial calendars or considering timely themes.

- Take a meeting with you or your client (casual meetings with one reporter can be called a "deskside" while more formal meetings with the editorial board may be in order for political campaigns).

- Link back to a pertinent blog post or page on your client's website relating to a topic they might be covering (SEO PR, covered in Chapter 10).

- Let your client pen an article for publication.

Press pitches provide more creative leeway than press releases and are a better option for getting out feature or trend stories over the typical news of the day. After reading my list of press release examples, you'll see that they generally represent your boring old water-cooler type news. However, you could also send a pitch to accompany a press release if you want to get more news out of your press release. None of my biggest wins were ever pitched via press release, they all came through an email pitch (likely preceded by a phone call). I don't think I have ever landed TV off of just a press release or advisory.

You really don't want to send too much in the way of words. The shorter the better. Assume everyone is reading emails (pitches) on their phone. Most importantly your pitch will change depending on the press medium. The unique way in which each medium reports the news must somehow be conveyed in your pitch, for example incorporating notes of sounds into radio pitches and visuals into TV pitches.

Your pitch ideas might come as we dig into each medium in the next section where I'll explain the inner-workings of each press category. Oftentimes, the pitch ideas answer the question: What are you asking the press for?

PHOTOS & VIDEOS

Did I mention that a picture tells a thousand words? I wonder if we've all been focusing on the wrong thing as PR professionals. Maybe it's the artistic creation of storytelling through photography and videography that is more important than developing our writing chops. If so, I am in deep trouble. I've always admitted I'm a terrible photographer.

That's why I'll often rely on the help of a professional photographer. Not only will print and online media sources run photos, with or without your press release or pitch, TV will even run photos or video taken by non-media members. Especially if they are interested in your story but don't have the staff to fully cover it.

Before explaining how to entice the media to use visual assets that I'll cover in Chapter 8, let's examine when we'd use a professional.

Some of the fancier magazines, like *Martha Stewart Living* and *O*, place a huge emphasis on photography, many times over content. Years back, I was trying to place some artisanal jams and hit the jackpot by getting access to a decision maker at *O*. She was a lovely lady who was stringing me along for months, saying they were considering placing the jams in the magazine. Even though I had included professional photos in every email pitch and mailed the actual product to editorial offices across New York City, she said the decision would come down to how their own photos of the product looked. Hiring the best photographer to shoot these jams would have been fruitless. *O* and similar magazines simply take, and publish, their own photos.

While I was able to place the jams in foodie magazines like *Bon Appetite* and *Cooking Light,* they never made it into *O* because of how *O*'s photographs of the jams turned out. The "story" about the jams was there. They were thoughtfully crafted out of charming Hood River, Ore., by local farmers who approached the work like how vintners make wine in Sonoma Valley. Moreover, it's not like any photographer couldn't figure out how to capture the jar's essence in just the right light. I suspect the jam's dated logo caused our demise. There was no way to get around a design that tried hard, but screamed 1980s.

This example illustrates that story isn't always everything. Even though we didn't get into *O*, we never would have gotten into the foodie mags without professional photos. So, you still need to hire a pro and attach one photo with every email when pitching products.

Here's when you'd want to hire a professional photographer:

- **Products:** Just hire a professional to shoot them, even if it's only once, please.

- **Events:** If you're asking people to pay to attend, you'll reap the rewards of having the event shot (at least through photography and possibly also hire a videographer, sometimes one professional can do both) during the first year, if not every year depending on budget and event scale. Use these assets to promote the event the following year.

- **Fundraisers:** If your event is a fundraiser full of mucky mucks, you might want a professional capturing who was there while also displaying the event's scale. Use these assets when announcing how much was raised, especially if you are asking people to pay to attend next year. Capturing your top sponsors and donors in their best light is also a good thing.

- **Headshots:** Get professional shots of really important executives or people you're highlighting in the news. Since these will be used over and over again, you — along with your subject's ego — will not regret it.

If we can't rely on a photographer or videographer's talent, we must do it ourselves. It can be done with a good quality smart phone. You can do it. I can do it. My grandma can do it. As long as a few simple rules are followed, explained in Chapter 8.

Photo Captions

When sending visuals to press, write a note saying who's in it, what they are doing and why. This is called a photo caption.

Not more than a few sentences, there is an art to writing a winning photo caption. List who's in the photo from left-to-right. Include job titles only if they are very important or you don't have much else to say. Definitely include organizations the people are with — it's a chance to get your organization's name included, along with any of your VIPs' organizations. I would consider VIPs to be top sponsors, donors, clients, or other people whose names lend you clout (typically politicians or public figures) or internal VIPs that you need to impress, such as your boss, executive leadership team or board members. If your picture depicts a large group of more than five people, identifying each person is unnecessary. Simply summarize who they are and what they're doing.

And finally, add a sentence that incorporates the results of what was happening in the photo if possible. X pounds of garbage collected; X dollars raised; or new office opened in X community.

You don't have a photo? I'm sorry. That is really too bad. Not only do most people look at the photos over reading the actual words of an article, you can get twice as much ink when you incorporate photos with text. Get used to taking them or directing others, even clients and bosses, to take them if you are unavailable.

BLOG POSTS

The New Press Release

Before Veracity, my husband and business partner worked in the digital marketing world, specifically in search engine optimization (SEO), which is the industry terminology meaning they try and get websites to rank higher in search engines like Google and Bing. Because of his digital savvy, we receive many new business leads from friends in the SEO industry.

As such, we've created a new sector of PR we've termed SEO PR. Many clients in this category are only interested in using PR as a means to increase their search results. They couldn't care less about getting a cover story in the *Wall Street Journal*, unless it is also on the famed newspaper's website, with a link leading back to their website.

That's because SEO involves getting links back to your website to drive traffic which shows Google you're the shit. I will explain more of the mechanics in Chapter 10, but know that garnering earned media coverage is a great way to do this.

More and more we have been relying on the blog post to drive SEO through PR. Writing a newsworthy blog post that incorporates industry trends and relevant statistics can fill in for the press release. If the post is full of key information, the media will have no choice but to link back to your post in any story they might do on the topic, driving important links back to your website, which is part of SEO PR.

> To learn more about my husband and business partner, Mike Rosenberg, listen to PR Talk podcast episode #49 on **PRtalk.co**

PRESS KITS & VIRTUAL PRESS ROOMS

Another famed PR tool is the press kit. There are a lot of misconceptions around this beauty. When I started at the second marketing agency I ever worked for — after breaking my first boss' heart to follow those exiting the revolving door my first agency had turned into — I headed toward larger pastures. This new agency was a full-fledged advertising firm, being the oldest ad shop in town. Headed by five partners, who's individual agencies had been purchased during their moment of weakness by the man at the helm, the agency was divided into four floors, with advertising account managers and the executive team on the first floor, copywriters and designers on the second and third floors and the PR and Public Affairs team hidden upstairs on the fourth floor — with honest-to-goodness secretaries scattered throughout. It was a modern day *Mad Men*.

I asked about putting a press kit together as I was handed my first account. I'd taken my new boss, Monique, by surprise. "You don't need a press kit for every client!," she said with the kind of flourish reserved for the most dramatic PR people of which she was one. I'm not sure I believed her at the time, suspecting she was embodying the quality I've come to abhor throughout my professional career — laziness.

However, over the course of the few years I was there, I realized she was right about this and many things. She was full of funny sayings she'd use to drive a professional lesson home. "Work smarter, not harder" was a phrase she used often and it aptly applies to this press kit instance. This job was the beginning of my understanding that not all PR is textbox. Not all clients and situations warrant the same treatment. Therefore, press kits can be created if there is enough to say.

If you've been working on your PR long enough you probably already have enough for a press kit. The topics I mentioned previously (fact sheets or media advisories) might be nice additions to the kit.

Basic Rundown of Press Kit Content Ideas:

- General fact sheet on the organization or event(s)

- General press release on whatever the news of the day is. This might be your rotating press release that is constantly updated with new information depending on what you're trying to promote.

  » For events this is the basic press release that offers the highlights in paragraph style

- Background sheets. You could have one for each of the following:

  » History/timeline

  » Top executives and/or board members and insight each person could offer the media

  » List of products with descriptions

  » List of services with descriptions

  » List of partners (charities, sponsors, etc.) with descriptions

- Infographics

- Photos

- Some people even put past press coverage in their press kits. I don't know if they are confused — thinking that press kits are used for audiences outside of the press. Or they are smartly thinking that their former media hits will give them credibility for future media kits. Whatever the case, it's not a bad idea.

> Make sure your contact information
> is on **every single document**.

The press kit lives online in this day and age. If you want to create a leave-behind in the form of printing out all of your releases and stuffing them into an old-school folder, like if you're doing a fancy press tour in New York, be my guest. Another Monique phrase comes to mind. "Maximize" anything you are doing. If you are spending the money to fly out to New York anyway, why not make a good impression with a nice leave-behind?

Moreover, you can forget the idea of throwing everything onto a thumb drive. Media contacts will just lose the thumb drive, never even bothering to look at it. It's another thing they'd have to hassle with. If the press kit is in a pretty folder that lives on their desk, or floor (in the case of my many messy media friends), their chances of spotting it, picking it up, pondering over it and eventually choosing to act on it are much higher.

Besides, anything important is going to live on your organization's website anyway. If you're going to the trouble of compiling a press kit, at the very least have it uploaded to a virtual press room on your website. A tangible thing actually doesn't exist until it's online. The worst thing that could happen is an important reporter remembering your pretty press kit — realizing one of the releases was perfect for a story — but they can't locate it amid the sea of press releases, press kits and media drops flying at them from PR people all over the world. They should be able to access your media kit online at a moment's notice.

MEDIA DROPS

Media drops are a fun way to grab the attention of media while also getting a good sense of where they work everyday. Think of a unique item to "drop" by newsrooms that is useful or interesting and somehow still speaks to your campaign goals. Include a personalized note, possibly with the press release or press kit attached.

Media drops were an extra last-minute action we'd take for a special event we were PR'ing during the time when I was working seven days a week, running PR for a multitude of fast-paced events at my first job. It was a fun way to get creative, see where my media friends worked, and most importantly stay in front of them.

The media drop should be exactly that — a "drop" by. You never ask to see the press contact as that would annoy them, but you hope to accidentally run into them, acting *oh so surprised*. Frequently visiting their places of work is a wonderful way to envision where the powers-that-be toil away at the demanding job of reporting the news. However, if you are far away or just too busy you can also have the item mailed to the contact.

Media drops could run the gamut from food or product samples, a technology gadget with your logo on it or something quirky that grabs their attention with the press release attached. But make it interesting or useful, please. While it's better to receive a gift attached to a press release, the media do get many little trinkets and tokens. Just take a trip into any local news station and you'll see the reporters' desks overflowing with junk delivered to them. You want to send something that will make all the other reporters stop in their tracks, wondering what that item is promoting. Be the talk of the newsroom!

SNAIL MAIL

Because all of us get so many emails now, the practice of email is becoming obsolete in some circles. But our industry will never completely turn verbal because humans can only keep so many details in their heads.

Things still need to be written down, so why not mail the documents? A radio show host recently told me that they NEVER get mail. Receiving an old-school letter might ensure that your press release is noticed before the 50,000 other releases that have been emailed in that day.

If you use a fancy media database software to track and maintain your media lists, you'll see that some savvy reporters have listed snail mail as their preferred method for PR people to reach out to them. This is an awesome way for media to weed out unworthy media pitches (and lazy PR people)!

THE TELEPHONE

Picking up the phone isn't as easy as it used to be. Did you know that the iPhone wasn't made to be used as a phone in the most traditional sense of the word? Meaning, held to the side of your face and spoken directly into. Instead it was made for more passive forms of engagement. Surfing. Posting. Texting. Emailing.

The actual conversation doesn't come in for some PR people until the bitter end of the pitch cycle, if at all. If you don't have the guts to call up a reporter, you might be in trouble. Sure it's important to lead with a solid email pitch, since they'll just ask for it anyway, but there will come a time when you have to bite the bullet and pick up the phone. I know it's intimidating but you didn't think I'd turn you loose without any media etiquette training did you?

> For a general conversation on PR tools, listen to
> PR Talk podcast episode #68 on **PRtalk.co**

CHAPTER FOUR

UNDERSTANDING THE MEDIA

There is a bear on the loose in Beaverton," he interjected into the middle of my phone pitch. Since Beaverton is a small local suburb of Portland, I knew this to be quite odd. "OK," I said while slamming down the phone. This wasn't rude of me at all, in fact hanging up on him was unexpectedly polite.

Whether you are a publicist, B2B'er or other, you'll be interacting with the media. Hold on to your seats because it's going to be a wild ride. The first thing to understand is that newsrooms operate differently than the traditional working environment. The faster the news is released, the more immediate the deadlines are and the lower the tolerance level for bullshit.

Let's say you're on the phone with Sally, a beloved legacy reporter who's been with your town's top station forever. When suddenly, mid-pitch, a shout floats across ten cubicles to land in Sally's ear, "I need the head-line ASAP." Rick's not being a jerk, he really does need it ASAP, so Sally hangs up on you because she knows that the newsroom just picked up a five-car crash from the police scanners only ten minutes before the next show is supposed to go live. Meanwhile, the producer is moving stories around in the day's line up — likely cutting the feel-good story pitched by a PR person about the zoo's pachyderm star giving birth to a baby calf — while the traffic helicopter reroutes to the scene and the anchor studies the new script.

You see, Rick had the story written for the web and just when he was about to write the story's headline he received pictures of the crash from the reporter in the sky just ten minutes before the show was to go on. He had to make a decision, upload the pictures or write the headline. Pictures tell a thousand words so he started in on the pictures. But he's no dummy, he glanced over at Sally, the diva reporter who's prime-time show isn't for two whole hours. A lifetime away. He yelled his request over the newsroom at her, "I need the headline!" Sally knew exactly who he was yelling at and what he needed. So she hung up on you to deliver the headline to the 24-year-old digital director without questioning it at all.

You'll need to quickly shed your sensitive skin and bear some rock-solid armor. This doesn't mean you should begin acting like a New York cabbie; just understand newsroom pressure and get over yourself.

MEDIA ETIQUETTE

Here are a few pointers that can help smooth out any rough press interactions:

Rule #1
Never and I mean NEVER fully launch into a pitch without asking if the person you're holding hostage has time to hear you out. The script below can help you ease into this transition.

Rule #2
Make your personal introduction brief. The media doesn't care if you're

employed by Cupcake PR firm, but representing Frosting Sauce company as your client. They also don't have time for your title and maybe even last name. The point is to get to the point, but in a casual way.

Your introduction could actually introduce your pitch topic so you can assess whether they will take your call while beginning your pitch at the same time. You've most likely emailed a pitch or press release and you're just calling to "follow up" — code for "what's the deal, are you covering my story or not?"

Pretend you are working for Entertainment Masters PR firm, representing the Traveling Clique Circus Extravaganza, which is rolling into town today. This "rolling into town" is a mini press event conveniently happening before the big event. All of the components of a live circus will unravel out of 12 large train cars. Clowns in mini cars. Lion tamers with their fiery rings. Livestock.

You of course sent out an email with the exact time and location of the "roll out," while painting the visual that's expected to unfold. But you know that your job is only half done after sending the email. It's time to follow up via phone. The words that come out of your mouth right now could be the most important words in the campaign. You are not with Entertainment Masters PR firm. You are not even with Traveling Clique Circus Extravaganza. You are simply with "the Circus."

Here is how I would combine Rule #1 and Rule #2 in a phone introduction:

> "This is <u>Amy</u> with the <u>Circus</u> calling about the **12 train cars that will roll into town today with clowns, lion tamers and livestock.** *Do you have a second?*"

There are four key elements to these short, but oh so important, two sentences.

1. **Amy:** you're briefly introducing who you are — who cares who you are really, this is just an unnecessary formality

that can even go away, but sometimes it's done by habit or can provide a mental warm up.

2. **Circus:** You're briefly stating whom you're with. We don't need the full client name, especially if it's a mouthful — that is what the press release is for.

3. **"Twelve train cars that will roll into town today with clowns, lion tamers and livestock":** This is your pitch. That's it. You've swiftly summarized what's going to happen while relying on a specific number (which the press loves) and a brief, but compelling, visual.

4. **"Do you have a second?":** Now you are no longer inconsiderate because you're pausing before going in for the kill. You're giving them ownership over their time, offering a choice to either hear you out or hang up the phone.

Getting a bit of the pitch in before you ask for their time is key because of course they have a second for something big. It's the news. However, what you think is important may not align with their needs at the moment of your call.

This pause allows space for them to recall what you've sent or to realize they may be missing out on something big. A sort of fumbling awkwardness typically occurs next, with them either saying they only have a minute — forever preserving time that is truly not their own while at work — or they begin searching for your press release in their mountainous in-box or attempt to mentally recall the important details, such as the expected time of the "roll in."

If they are physically or mentally searching during this pause, this gives you time to continue your pitch in a real causal, non-overbearing way. The causal sound of your voice is key because it shows you are cool, you are not going to keep them on the phone, you get it. You have the press release right in front of you and you're reminding them when it is and you're possibly forwarding it to them again so that you don't have to wonder if they received it. Hopefully it bubbles up to the top of their in-box while you've got them on the phone so you can be sure they received it and they might even offer their intentions — whether they will cover it or not.

Rule #3

Do what they ask of you. If they ask you to call them back at a certain time — do it. If they need you to scrounge up more information — do it. When pitching a potential story, you're asking a lot of them. The least you could do is oblige with their timeline and get them everything they need.

Rule #4

Deliver on your promises. Do not dangle the CEO as a potential interview before realizing she's wintering in Baja for the month. Make sure you can hold up your end of the bargain before offering interviews. Find out who's around to represent your organization before sending your news out. Hold your executives accountable. Connect with them first to make sure you can offer them as interviews, you might even get their schedule at the same time. And if they bail on you during your time of need — be a big boy or girl and set things straight for the next time around. A flaky executive could damage your reputation with the media.

Rule #5

Be easy to reach after sending out any kind of news. Of course place your contact information front and center in the communication — always keeping your phone with you and on. Again, most media won't "schedule a time to talk." When they want something, they want it now, assuming your timing is right, which is everything. You started this, so stick around to see it through.

Rule #6

Never follow up more than two times with the exact same pitch to the exact same contact. But I'm not telling you to completely drop it if you aren't getting any love. It's a sign that something is not working and you either need to change contacts or change your approach by updating your story angle, pitch or release. Or just drop it altogether.

MEDIA EXCLUSIVES

Sometimes you'll only send your idea to your top media contact. This is called "pitching an exclusive." With a media exclusive, you're promising your contact has the first right of refusal to your news. If your contact agrees to write a story, media exclusives ensure you won't share the news with anyone else until after your contact has had their fill with it. Playing favorites is OK because it entices your contact to take you and your story seriously. You might not get coverage from anyone else, but at least some coverage is guaranteed if your contact agrees.

The number one media exclusive rule is this: wait to hear back from your contact before you go all over town promising exclusives or be clear about when you are going to offer it up to others. You MUST NOT pitch exclusives on the same story simultaneously. Once you get a "no," you're free to move on to the next contact. This may require you to make a couple of phone calls. But if you get the coveted "yes," you need to courteously wait until your contact has their story fleshed out and is ready for you to share the news with their competition, unless you've been clear about the intended general release date. Help your contact by providing access to sources and all the materials they are requesting.

Media exclusives allow you to hold leverage over the willing media contact. Meaning, you can ask them to cover your story in a certain light. Don't be too obvious and bossy, but if you make your intentions clear up front, you can ask them to speak with a certain source, include a specific statistic or link to a selected website. It's sort of like a "you scratch my back; I'll scratch your back" situation. Just be reasonable. Again, clearly state reasonable intentions in the beginning.

CHANGING RULES
FOR DIFFERING MEDIA

While the media etiquette rules apply to all types of media, the way you relate to your contacts, and the timing of how you reach out will change depending on the type of outlet — print/online, online only, TV, radio and new forms of media, such as podcasting. To get really good at your job, you must understand each media type, specifically what their newsroom staff titles mean and how their news cycle timelines work.

Timelines

I'll say it again — timing is everything. Perhaps it's more important than getting your story just right. Releasing your news during the most opportune time can increase its success a million-fold. There isn't a one-fits-all solution to determining timelines for the various mediums, so we'll go in-depth with each medium in the upcoming chapters.

Understanding what kind of medium your news fits can help narrow your focus, set your plan of action and present the possibilities. In some instances, you'll be too late with your news. This is fine for learning purposes, but eventually the press timelines should live within you as a working part of your brain. Understanding each medium's intricate timelines until they instinctively inform your decisions is part of living the maximized PR lifestyle.

Timing concerns come in all shapes and sizes. How far ahead of the deadlines do you need to be? Can you be too early? When is the best time to follow up? I've attempted to guide you in the upcoming chapters, but you'll need to discover how your unique contacts and outlets work, shaping your customized schedules.

Staff Titles

You must have working knowledge of press titles and what they mean. How else would you know whom to contact if you don't know what their role is? Press titles are getting a little murky over here in Oregon with *The Oregonian's* fancy titles for journalists and editors. *The Oregonian* is my state's largest "daily" newspaper, which doesn't deliver to doorsteps daily anymore, instead delivering news to our computer screens on the daily — if not by the minute — so I guess that's how it's justified in calling itself a daily newspaper.

The funky titles found at papers like *The Oregonian* illustrate how they are trying to shed old-school print-first ways by communicating their digital-savviness through a litany of confusing titles. With murky titles you'll have to read between the lines, for example determining that the managing producer title is actually the editor. If you've been in PR awhile you might know managing producer is an odd title at a newspaper. But with everything being online — including video at a traditionally print outlet — the title conveys the managing producer (otherwise known as the editor) is also overseeing those digital items for either the entire newspaper or a specific section of the newspaper. But again, we have to start somewhere so just learning what it is that the editor does — to determine if you need to be connecting with them or their reporter — can be a good jumping off point.

BUILDING YOUR MEDIA LIST

The media list is a living, breathing entity that the PR person works with every day. Think of it as a verb. List maintenance is an ongoing task, never completed. Newsrooms all over the world are constantly evolving — cutting sections, departments and shows, while adding (or not adding) new, slightly updated sections, departments and shows.

If I am working in my hometown I am guilty of keeping the list in my head. Dangerous. You need to have it in some sort of program that can be easily accessed and shared if necessary. Even if you work alone, you may need to share the list one day with a client or colleague. Moreover, the list organizes you. Without it you will forget a contact, maybe one that you don't view as important, but they are all important in their own way.

Media list building typically looks like a combination of researching each media outlet's website, along with using the resources of a media software database.

Using Media Software to Build Lists

If you do not have the finances for media database software — we currently use Cision which *reportedly* provides access to all the media contacts in the world — don't worry because they just provide a starting point. Most of them are fairly useless anyway because you will likely be constantly confirming and changing the contacts based on what the publication says about itself on its own website. However, the media databases provide a good starting point for high profile outlets, such as *Martha Stewart* or *Time* magazine, where they do not list their roster of reporters online. Even if the contacts aren't 100 percent correct, media databases at least provide some names and phone numbers. Begin your list building by reaching out to those in the database and refine from there.

The way I work with a media database is of course to build media lists the opposite way everyone else tells me I should. They understandably say to search by contacts. They say if you are working in Atlanta for the first time, just run a search of all the editors in Atlanta and you'll turn up everything you need. The publications would be listed behind each editor's name, so you'll find out what outlets are available to you that way. Not good enough.

As we discussed before, outlets don't follow the traditional mode of title-bestowing these days.

What if an important daily newspaper in Atlanta is over boring old titles like editor, electing for titles such as managing producer or just your standard editor-in-chief or managing editor, completely bypassing the straight-forward editor title? You could possibly miss the most important news outlet in town!

That's why I build the list of outlets first and then pull up the list of contacts falling under each outlet and hand-select the contacts I want to reach out to from that outlet. I often include multiple people from each outlet in the media list and send group emails to the selected contacts at each outlet. For instance, you may think you've found the perfect reporter to send your story to, but you might also want to cc the editor just in case that person has been reassigned to another "beat" (journalism jargon for the topic that reporter typically covers) or is out sick. The larger the outlet, the more likely you'll want to cc some type of underling as well — anyone with the name assistant or associate in front of the word editor will do. The editor at a larger organization may be too busy to catch every last email flooding the in-box.

Using Online Searches to Build Lists

I then double check my media database through an online search, making sure I've got all the pertinent outlets for my particular campaign. While it might take a little bit more time, Google is quickly usurping the role of the media database. You can find lost publications through Google and once you have them, you can often access a better list of contacts through each outlets' online roster, which are sometimes updated more frequently than the media databases.

I find that most average outlets do a great job of explaining themselves on their websites. Go to the "about" page for a general idea of what they cover and then somewhere not overly obvious they should have a roster of contacts, including editors and reporters. This could be hidden deeper within the "about" section or it could be within the "contact us" section. If emails and phone numbers aren't listed, some additional general sleuthing should turn that gold up.

Then you might even dig further to uncover what your target media contacts are covering either online, in print or on-air. Getting a feel for each contact's tone and interests can not only help you build a bulletproof list, but also enable you to tailor your pitches.

And again, in a perfect world, I'm constantly updating my lists as I go about my work each day.

Organizing Your Media Lists

If organized properly, lists can rearrange your thoughts so that you remember to switch language between audiences. Separate each audience into different lists or tabs within the same list. If you are operating at maximum capacity, TV, radio, print, social and online should get their own slightly different pitch. Having them in different lists can help you do that more efficiently through mail merges in Google Sheets or exporting through a software.

The ultimate maximizers don't even rely on tools like mail merges and exporting because they can't! They are already in conversation about other things with their contacts so it would be weird to send a blanket, general email to them. They have to ask their media contacts what they are going to bring to Ricky's potluck tomorrow, what they thought about their other client's recent op-ed submission, and most importantly do they think Ricky's new girlfriend will be at the potluck? Ideally, after a while you've spent so long building relationships, you adjust your tone, message and request through each customized email.

CHAPTER FIVE

WORKING WITH PRINT & ONLINE

Since there are so many different types of print media, we're not in a one-size-fits-all situation. Also, understand that print and online media are often the same. Many print stories also end up on the organization's website, and sometimes extra reporting from the organization is slated for their online channels, never even making it into the print version. This extra online reporting can allow for looser — or more immediate, whichever way you want to look at it — deadlines.

As with anything in PR, each outlet will have its own way of doing things, online and offline, so just because I've outlined timelines for specific types of print, take them as a general guide. You could even customize timelines down to the individual contact level, remembering that each media member will also have their own way of doing things. Committing your media market's quirkiness to memory will eventually inform your planning — another example of fine-tuning the PR mindset.

Here's a general breakdown of the main types of print media, with an understanding that online media will sometimes either follow or operate independently of print.

PRINT MEDIA:
TYPES & TIMELINES

Daily Newspapers

Daily newspapers are mostly looking for news affecting their coverage area. While the big national conglomerates, like *USA Today*, pick up national/international news, the capacity of some "dailies" could be as minute as covering just a portion of the state in which they are located. But most cover the news within their entire home state, mixed with the top regional, national and international news.

Timelines: Your typical daily news is working in real-time, so timelines are pretty much day of, day before or a few days before for general news. A features or investigative reporter might take their time uncovering every angle within a piece, so you might not have a hard and fast deadline to abide by with them, other than "hurry up and wait." However, aiming to get after anyone at a daily about three weeks ahead can help you stay on the safe side, but you'll probably have to follow up with them because that much ahead would be a little on the early side.

Special Sections

Daily newspapers may put out special sections that run:

- Weekly — such as a special insert on entertainment every weekend: Aim to get information to them three weeks ahead.

- Once or a few times/year — like a holiday gift guide: Aim to get the information to them roughly three months ahead, but know that your "drop dead" is likely six weeks ahead.

  » Special sections such as these should be listed in the newspaper's editorial calendars. You'll learn how to use editorial calendars to plan ahead later in this chapter.

Local/Community Newspapers

These could cover the news within a neighborhood or local community. They are always looking for news that directly relates to their specific readership or the location their readership is in. Community newspapers are typically produced on a monthly or weekly schedule, however some larger areas may put out community rags that are distributed a couple times a week. Capturing these details in a customized media list that ages well will help you understand how to plan and execute your PR.

Timelines:

- Monthlies: Aim to get the information to them two months ahead, but three weeks ahead would be your deadline.

- Weeklies: Aim to get the information to them three weeks ahead, but know that your "drop dead" is about one or two weeks ahead.

Monthly City or Statewide Lifestyle Magazines

These more entertainment-based magazines cover fun things to do in their area as well as more features-based news, including in-depth profiles of local influencers or current events that aren't so current anymore because their news is about a month late.

All media outlets experience the problem of the internet breaking news before traditional forms of communication. That's why most outlets also have websites, blogs and social media channels to release quick news on. Some outlets strictly designate themselves as in-depth features or profile-focused organizations, safely staying away from the breaking news game.

Timelines: Aim for three months ahead but six weeks ahead would be your deadline. Even though they are monthlies, just like the monthly local community papers mentioned above, they typically spend a little more time on their stories and visuals, thus needing additional time to work with your information.

Quarterlies

I hate these! Since they only come out four times each year, they are so hard to plan for in advance. However, the planning can and should be done because they are often very special publications that meet a specific purpose and serve a designated audience, such as wedding planning or regional travel.

Timelines: It's going to be a grueling six to eight months ahead. Yes, it's hard to know what you would even pitch. You'll want to think in terms of big seasonal ideas here.

Fancy Monthly Magazines

This is how I designate the biggies (such as *Forbes* or *Shape*), mainly coming out of New York, but serving a nationwide audience. You can even consider a narrow focus publication, like *Food & Wine*, to fall under this category since its published out of New York, yet it reaches a mass nationwide audience.

Timelines: Six months ahead but you can sneak in around five months ahead. Know that the months move quickly in PR. You start the press contact work around six months and finally get to the right source in the nick of time around five months ahead. I know that it doesn't make sense that the statewide monthly magazine timelines are shorter, but nothing in PR is ever black and white. These really fancy magazines take themselves really seriously — likely because they have massive audiences and advertising dollars.

Trade and Vertical Publications

What qualifies as a trade or a vertical media source for you depends on what you happen to be representing at the moment. Let's say I'm a PR firm that works with a lot of construction companies and is trying to get more construction clients. My trades would be what directly relate to my industry (PR in this case) and my verticals are what directly relate to where I'm trying to be seen (construction in this case).

You could even think of consumer press targets in the form of a main, constant audience (trade) and specially targeted audiences for individual messages or unique circumstances (verticals).

Timelines: Generally start the work three months ahead, but you might be fine at two months ahead. After awhile, you should understand the inner workings of your trades and verticals as they are like their own mini-industries. Hopefully you'll begin to realize when you are pitching too early and when the timing is just right.

PRINT & ONLINE NEWS STAFF TITLES

Editor

This person is in charge of what the paper puts out on a broad scale, nearing the minutiae. The larger the outlet, probably the less often they'll hand-select each story, with their own reporters bringing stories to their attention that they either accept or decline. This leaves the editor room to set the larger editorial picture. In general, the editor has the last say on most things, from big items to what sentence goes where.

Reporter

In most instances, it's probably best to uncover what each reporter focuses on and pitch the reporter directly because it's not like the editor is standing behind a curtain like the Wizard of Oz attempting to assign stories. Most reporters are deeply invested in their particular "beat," bringing key stories within their assigned area of interest to the forefront.

However, it's not a bad idea to cc the editor if you are unsure. This isn't overbearing, it's a safeguard to give your story a better chance of getting in the right hands. If the reporter is out sick, the editor will know which reporter to pass it off to. Also, the best media database software can't track the frequent changes happening in newsrooms across the world, but each individual editor can track their own internal changes.

Notice I said cc the editor. Do not bcc editors or other reporters to an email. You want to direct your email specifically to one person and let the other people that also work at this outlet know that you sent it in case your primary contact is unavailable or not the correct contact.

Managing Editor

Larger publications will have this. I have a hard time discerning the difference between the plain old editor and the managing editor, but what I can come up with is that the managing editor is in charge of who is doing what in their newsroom, while the editor is in charge of editing the "copy" (industry jargon for words on a page).

In an important, large organization, let's say *Cosmopolitan* magazine, I'd float the story idea by the managing editor first to avoid wading through a sea of confusing titles and incorrect online descriptions before pitching. They should be able to at least send you to the starting line.

Editor in Chief/Editor at Large

These are some of the top dogs. You typically can't get stories placed through these people as they are too high up, therefore leave them alone. However, titles can sometimes be deceiving. It's really important to pull up the roster of who's working at the publication you're pitching. The "Editor in Chief" may be the only editor on staff managing a newsroom of two freelance reporters. In this case, they would be your main contact.

This is why I do not rely on a media database to build my media list. I can use the names and titles that the database puts in front of me as a starting point, but I have to see the whole newsroom roster to under-stand what I'm really dealing with. Sometimes the editor in chief also owns the publication and acts as the reporter and publisher, selling ads as well. Hiding from PR people behind the publisher title is sheer genius.

Publisher

If the editor in chief is the top dog, the publisher *could be* the alpha wolf, depending on the publication. The publication actually doesn't have to be that large for the publisher to be the most important piece of the organization because it sometimes signifies that they are the owner — the ultimate boss. In general, the publisher is in charge of the publication's overall financial success, tasked with ensuring advertising and subscription revenue surpass the cost of operating the publication. Their duties could be as wide-ranging from managing a large staff to pounding the pavement in pursuit of the next advertiser.

Again, it's important to glean a clear understanding of the inner-work-ings of each publication. If the publication is a one-stop shop, the publisher might be your gal or guy. But for the most part they typi-cally won't be.

Digital Editor/Producer

This person is either in charge of throwing all print content into some sort of digital format — whether it is a fun social media post or decid-ing that the breaking news of the day needs to trump the other homep-age stories — or they create their own content only for digital platforms. Most often this role is doing a combination of both.

This contact can be a godsend if you're running late with your story submission, which can happen to the best of us, especially when a cli-ent or boss doesn't understand our deadlines, bringing news to us late. Or at the same time, you can rely on this contact to get better online placement and more social sharing for a piece that you worked on with a traditional print reporter. For SEO PR this may be your most important contact.

You might be thrown off by the example I used in the beginning of this chapter about *The Oregonian's* managing producer titles. The reason they don't have just a digital editor/producer on staff is because the entire newsroom works their stories into an online format, possibly in a different way than they would for print. So, since it isn't really a one or the other situation, possibly the vague titles depicting the collision of print and online make sense.

MORE ABOUT ONLINE NEWS

The immediacy of web-based PR offers a flexibility that I love. The fast-paced work of online press means that in most cases the deadline was yesterday. Rather, there aren't any deadlines as you must almost begin to predict the future. Of course this isn't always the case when it comes to digital outlets that aren't solely focused on current news — such as business, health, or fashion — but they may also have a breaking news section because they can.

Their platform is so immediate, they can augment stories that have already been posted, morph their coverage to fit what's going on and change direction at the drop of a hat. However, they too are working toward a specific mission, with feature articles and stories that fit a specific season or event. That work takes a lot of planning and organization. So much so, that some websites and blogs even release editorial calendars to assist your advance planning.

Again, most of the publications and broadcast outlets you gain placement in also have blogs, websites or social media. Many outlets operate both their print and digital news sources in the most mundane way possible — by simply reusing what was printed in the paper on their digital channels. Therefore, in many instances you almost have a guarantee that your stories will also make it online if they have already landed in print.

This is so true that I mix up the words print and digital constantly in speech. My firm has probably been passed over for work because of this. Potential clients of the hip variety are thinking, who is this woman that keeps talking about publications and print? Is she stuck in the 90s? No. It's the opposite. Getting digital PR today is such a given that it's not even in my vernacular. Web-based PR is so essential that we'll frequently pass on pitching media outlets that do not have websites or do not include links to clients' websites in their stories. For clients who are using PR primarily as a means to increase their website's visibility in search engines (aka SEO), the reasons to appear in just print may be so insignificant that we don't even waste our time. Many search experts have called earned media coverage the most powerful form of true organic search engine marketing possible. For this reason my firm specializes in a new form of PR we have coined "SEO PR" (Chapter 10).

Online News Timelines

For the most part, I would say that the deadline for current news websites that pump out content on the daily (or the hourly) would be one to two days ahead, but it depends. Get to know your sources. When are the new stories published? When are the email newsletters delivered to your in-box? Match your deadlines to the print timelines but know there's a little more wiggle room online. If an online writer takes a month to put a story together, approach this like a monthly newspaper, pitching about six weeks ahead. If an email newsletter is sent out weekly, pitch it about three weeks ahead.

WHAT TO PITCH PRINT & ONLINE

You've learned about the different types of print, which you've seen by now could also mean online, and who works there. Now you must decide what to pitch. If you aren't going to send a press release about one of the sample news topics outlined in Chapter 2, here is where the media pitch comes in.

Remember that you are asking for something within the pitch, typically for story coverage. You might have the original story idea, which would incorporate your organization in the pitch, or you might know what stories your media target is already working on and the goal of your pitch is to get them to include your organization somehow.

Beyond keeping your pitch concise and clear, ensure that your pitch is either newsworthy or timely — by tying into current industry or consumer trends or providing a source to offer upcoming market predictions.

You could also incorporate your organization into one of the below possibilities through an email pitch:

- Editorial Calendars
- Contributed Articles
- Blog Posts (SEO PR)

EDITORIAL CALENDARS

Editorial calendars are a good excuse for media pitches. You may have heard of editorial calendars in the realm of content marketing, with a calendar used to track who is blogging and when. But traditional print publishers first used editorial calendars to manage the publication of books, magazines and newspapers.

Many print publications rely on editorial calendars — otherwise known as "Ed Cals" — to map out what they will cover and when. Beyond helping editorial departments plan in advance, advertising departments use them to sell their ads, providing a "FOMO" type of nudge.

FOMO stands for "Fear of Missing Out." Pretend you represent a real estate company, handling the advertising, PR, the whole schabang. A top publication calls you, saying this April is our real estate focus because everyone knows that the real estate market really heats up in the springtime. "Competitor A and Competitor B will be advertising in this issue, so you might not want to miss out," the advertising rep says.

Well, of course you don't want to miss out. You loathe Competitor A with a vengeance for taking your top real estate agent away. Competitor B has the most sales in the marketplace, which shouldn't be the case because it is your mission to create such powerful marketing that your company tops the charts. But then you remember you're a startup without any financing. You take a deep breath, put one foot in front of the other, and start somewhere.

What the advertising rep isn't telling you is that the editorial department will be creating stories around real estate in April. This is your salvation! Not only is getting included in these stories "free," you remember that the public understands published stories to be more credible and reliable than ads. Press coverage like this offers more of a chance for startups to finally prove to everyone they do know what they are talking about.

Ed Cals are the PR person's best friend because they essentially offer a sneak peek into what each media outlet is covering. We'll examine how to find and pitch them.

How to Find Ed Cals

Make no mistake. The media won't help you by directing you to these hidden jewels, you'll have to hunt for them. Ed Cals are typically found in the advertising section of a media outlet's website, in the Media Kit. The Media Kit is everything a media outlet could ever fathom to put in one place to sell you an ad. It has circulation and demographic statistics, pricing, pictures and graphs. Way down at the bottom are the Ed Cals, and that's where the savvy PR people go.

Sometimes the Ed Cals are nowhere to be found, not even in the Media Kit. If you find this to be the case, just email a contact in the advertising department and ask for the Ed Cal. You might explain that you are just a PR person and aren't looking to place an ad so you don't get an eager phone call. If you still get that eager phone call, just play nice, they could bring insider media connections to you. This is rare. More often, it's beneficial for PR people to go rogue. If your pitch comes through the advertising department it might stink of dirty dollar bills even if you have no plans of spending any advertising budget with them. You still need to be nice.

Now, if you've perused the Media Kit and contacted the advertising department for the Ed Cals and they say they don't have any, well, that's that. There are no Ed Cals. Move on.

How to Use Ed Cals

Armed with the Ed Cals, now is the time to roll up your sleeves and get to work planning. Here are the steps I recommend for Ed Cal organization:

- Save the Ed Cals in a file on your computer relating to the topic.

- Cull through them in search of anything that could be related to the organization or cause you're repping.

- Create a calendar of stories you plan to target. I put the calendar in a Google Sheet and include the following:

  » Name of outlet

  » Issue release date

  » Article topic and details

  » Deadline, if listed. If not, take a guess. See PR Timelines section.

  » Contact, this may be listed somewhere in the media kit. If not, take another guess. See Media Titles section.

  » Status section. This is where I hold myself accountable and list all the actions I've taken on each particular article, from my first point of contact to finally landing the article.

- Include the deadline to pitch your targeted story in your personal/client calendar. The Ed Cal could very well bring you multiple articles to pitch for one client or topic so you might consider putting a standing monthly date in your calendar, pinging you to check the Ed Cal list and pitch what's coming up.

How to Pitch Using Ed Cals

There are many ways you could go about pitching the ideas found within Ed Cals. Each type of outlet has its own way of doing things. This could vary from outlet to outlet, or it could be standard across the many outlets within that trade or vertical.

Take the work we've been doing for a top nutritional supplement company for almost a decade. Since they rely on their manufacturers to get their product into the hands of consumers, our audience is decision makers and scientists within the supplement manufacturing industry.

Such a highly specialized audience reads its own little pocket of publications, websites and newsletters that work in a straightforward manner that's similar among each outlet. Every month a calendar notice pops up, reminding us to send pitches based on our Ed Cal research.

All we have to do is open up the Ed Cal Google Sheet and review the opportunities for that month we've already researched and organized. We then simply contact the opportunities with a clear, short pitch that includes the article topic and date of issue we're referencing in the email subject line so everyone can stay organized. When we put this information up front and center in the subject line, our media contacts know the email is relevant. If we have anything new to say — for this client it would be directing the press target to a new study that pertains to the article we're inquiring about — we'll include that in the pitch. But since funding scientific studies is very expensive, many times we don't have anything new to reference. That's OK. We still reach out and offer our client as a resource. More times than not we're included as a contact point.

And this is the best part. The media contact then emails their questions to us, which we then send to our client, our client answers the questions to the best of their ability — we have a heck of a time wrangling through the mix of broken English and weird science language as we edit — and then we send it back to the press contact (after gaining approval from the client on our changes of course). We garner reams of press coverage each year with this simple system, only putting out a press release when it warrants, which is like two times a year. This is high quality secretarial work in its finest.

How to Write the Ed Cal Media Pitch

At the very forefront, your pitch serves the purpose of getting the Ed Cal article topic back on the media contact's radar, bringing it to their attention at the most ideal time if they've forgotten about the upcoming story topics, since the Ed Cals are created at the start of the year. At the same time, you're offering a source to add commentary or expert opinion to the story. Include a few sentences about why they should consider your source and what your organization or the source can offer on the specific topic. Link to more information, such as referenced studies or other details to further your point. If I'm an editor assigning a story about trends in pharmaceutical formulations, I don't really care if your CFO has won an award relating to sound financial practices. If she has something compelling to say about pharmaceutical formulations, that will make me want to talk with her.

If you don't know who is writing the story, pitch the editor or person in charge of the newsroom; they'll point you in the right direction.

If you aren't already on a first-name basis with the editors, you may have to work a little more diligently to prove yourself in the beginning.

This doesn't necessarily mean creating a longer pitch. When you're trying to build a relationship and establish article inclusion, you'd ideally bring new info to the table. This could range from studies pointing to new findings, trendspotting, up-and-comers in the field, to new products and services. Basically, what is new and interesting is the name of the game.

Consumer Publication Ed Cals

I've been writing about business and scientific-related outlets a lot in this section because my work relies on Ed Cals for B-to-B (business to business) PR work, but Ed Cals can also help you make inroads with consumer publications. Many of the top lifestyle, health, travel, cooking, parenting, etc., outlets rely on Ed Cals to map out their editorial coverage for the year as well.

Follow the same steps previously outlined, but keep two things in mind:

1. Pictures really do tell 1,000 words in this instance. Your pitch might follow the same format as what I previously outlined, but invest in high-quality photos, especially if you are pitching a product.

2. Be open to other suggestions. On your quest to get your Ed Cal pitch in front of the right person, you might be pointed in a different direction. Remember that everyone you speak with at a large consumer publication is your friend. You get Lacy on the line and discover that your Ed Cal pitch doesn't work right now. But while you were chatting with Lacy, the conversation veered into a different product. Lacy's ears perked up because this other product fits seamlessly into the story Jane is working on. Look at that! Now you have an introduction to your new source, Jane, or at the very least you'd start your pitch to Jane name-dropping your new best friend, Lacy!

I suppose the two points above could be kept into consideration for all kinds of outlets, but I want you to keep an open mind with consumer outlets, and perhaps try a little harder because they are a different beast.

What Types of Ed Cals to Horde

Of course you've done your research and are only considering outlets that your demographic would be interested in. These could range from:

- Consumer outlets that your demographic would read for any consumer-facing PR campaign.

- Trade and vertical outlets, if you are trying to reach a business audience.

As previously explained, trade outlets represent the industry you work within. For people reading this book, their "trades" are probably marketing and/or PR.

Vertical outlets would be a side industry you are trying to do business in or currently do business in, such as pharmaceuticals for me. For instance, I own and operate a PR firm so my main trade would be PR. However, many of the industries that I am trying to do business in, such as pharmaceuticals and supplements in the case of this chapter, would be my "verticals."

For more on editorial calendars, listen to
PR Talk podcast episode #9 on **PRtalk.co**

CONTRIBUTED ARTICLES

If a particular theme is emerging in an industry (industry trend) that your organization could offer thoughts, tips or advice on, rather than simply pitching that the press write the story, you could suggest that a "source" from your organization write an article about it — to be published in print or online. There are many names for the kinds of articles that are written by an outside source and published in newspapers, websites/blogs or magazines, including:

Contributed or Bylined Article

This is a fast way to say that an expert outside of the media outlet will pen the article. The author's, and hopefully organization's, name would also appear in the byline of the contributed article.

Op-Ed

This is short for "opposite the editorial page," as these opinion pieces are usually printed on the opposite page of the editorial section where newspaper editors rant about issues. Written by people outside of the media outlet, they are found in many of the daily newspapers across the nation. This type of article should also include the author's name and organization.

Letter to the Editor

This is just what it sounds like. A letter to a newspaper or magazine editor that is printed either in the front or the back of the publication. It's a great way to get your organization's message or viewpoint on an issue in front of the public. And depending on the publication, you could have a lot of leeway or just a little leeway in how blatantly you pose your message. Your state's top daily newspaper isn't going to run just anything, which is why your letter must be related to the news of the day and not a sales pitch. However, other outlets will run just about anything, therefore you're allowed more freedom.

Where Does the Media Pitch Come In?

In a perfect world, I wouldn't write the article without knowing that I at least have someone interested in running it. So sometimes I'll send a pitch that's as short as three to five sentences asking if they are interested in running a piece written by (insert important sounding executive name and title here with credible organization) on x, y, z topic.

If I have more information at the ready, I'll go into depth without caring how much time I'm spending because I'll likely reuse the pitch copy in the article. I'll begin with a short, compelling first paragraph to hook them into the topic, and then I'll likely list statistics backing up my expert's opinion or providing more background in bullet point form.

Topics you could pitch for contributed articles include:

- Market trends — delivering insight into a particular market or micro-economy. If your expert is truly informed, you could land a quarterly, or even monthly publishing schedule.

- Opinions — on current international, national, local, or industry news and how various outcomes would relate to your customers or service population, if they are representative of the audience of that particular outlet.

- Hot consumer topics — for instance, gut health is all the rage now in diet for nutrition-related clients, or bringing mindfulness into your movement practice for exercise-related clients.

———

PR professionals and the organizations they represent shouldn't expect payment from the media for delivering content. Sure, outlets will pay freelancers to write full articles for them, but contributed pieces are different. Typically around 800 to 1,000 words, they skim the surface of any issue — sometimes just stating your organization's opinion or educating readers about what's going on. You wouldn't necessarily delve into an issue by interviewing external sources nor extensively researching. This is the epitome of the "you scratch my back, I'll scratch your back" situation that is a constant theme running through PR. The media knows you want your organization's and executive's name in lights, while you know they're looking for credible content.

"GHOSTWRITING"

A Frequent Result of Pitching Contributed Articles

Most PR people end up writing the article on behalf of their expert. Yes, you heard me right. The most insightful, eloquent pieces you'll ever write may have another person's name gracing the byline. If doing all the work without any of the glory leaves you feeling like a slighted Cinderella, welcome to PR. Our job is to push other people into the spotlight and then silently take a backseat.

That role can be relevant in many situations beyond ghostwriting. Not only is your job about garnering earned media for an organization or cause, it's also about presenting it in the best, most persuasive light. One way to do that is by stepping back and letting someone with a more reputable title — most often from the C-suite — serve as the spokesperson.

Most people know that the PR person is behind the most effective writing. The press knows this, your management team knows this, and if your boss doesn't know this, what are you doing? Of course somehow, you need to let the powers that be know that you wrote the article. And, if you ever end up looking for a new job, be sure to add the article donning someone else's name to your portfolio — telling your interviewers that you actually wrote, and hopefully placed, that article.

Of course nothing in PR is black and white, so you'll likely run across the whole gamut of ghostwriting situations over the course of your career. Sometimes working with your expert, or "author," is most challenging. Here are a few scenarios:

Expert Who Writes Well

You may have hit the jackpot with an expert that's not only a good writer, but actually understands how to write for the press while putting thought and care into the articles you're landing for them. This is rare, because often experts are busy and not always polished writers. Hold on tightly to this dream situation because you'll be able to land more placements with the extra time it affords you.

"Helpful" Expert Who Isn't Helping

This is pretty much the worst case scenario because this person wants to remain in control and can greatly lengthen or confuse the process. Let's hone in on the various personality types that frequently arise:

- Unreliable — the work may not be a top priority since it falls under PR.

- Knowledgeable but confusing — their knowledge doesn't help if it's presented oddly.

- Not experts — yes, many people climb the executive ranks without much understanding of what they are supposed to be experts about.

- Bad writers — their writing is so bad that it would have been faster for you to start from scratch without their "help."

These scenarios will teach you to remain in charge of writing the article because colleagues like these could very well cost you the article placement. There isn't anything more disappointing than landing a killer placement that isn't coming to fruition.

If you're at an agency and believe you don't have enough budget [time allotted] to place AND write an article for a particular client, you might be saying goodbye to your client or job with this attitude. Maybe it wasn't meant to be or they were a nightmare client anyway. But sometimes you have to go over-budget, whether that's extra time spent on the client or pulling a few late nights if you're in-house. If you are at an agency, I don't mean going over-budget in the sense that you'd charge extra for this. Rather, I'm proposing you eat the cost in extra time spent. What good are you to anyone with a bunch of media interest without placements?

Show your client or boss that you can get a few of these placed, let them bask in the glory of seeing their name in print and then cut the cord by informing them you need more budget (if you're at an agency) or you need a freelance writing budget (if you're in-house).

Expert Who Bestows Their Knowledge

It's helpful if your expert at least has some basis of knowledge to offer. With busy experts, all you have to do is get them on the phone for a conversation about the topic you've landed, take copious notes, and augment those notes into an article. You can try to conduct an email interview, but sometimes I find that this either intimidates people into thinking they have to write a whole bunch of stuff for you so they never get around to doing it, or they end up writing a jumble of a mess that isn't helpful because it takes you longer to weed through it than just writing it yourself.

Phone conversations are best because if your expert is truly an expert, they will explain the topic to you in great detail so you can learn along the way. You are just the writer in this case serving as the conduit of their knowledge to the public. If your expert arms you with enough knowledge, you hardly even have to use your brain.

Moreover, the current editor of the *Portland Business Journal*, Suzanne Stevens, told me in a PR Talk podcast interview (PRtalk.co) that the best interview answers come from follow-up questions. I must have known this all along and it's why I've leaned heavily on real conversations, rather than email, for my most substantial writing work.

Watch this video about getting information out of your thought leader on **PRtalk.co**. Even though it is geared toward credit unions, you'll find parallels with any industry.

BLOG POSTS

While any contributed article can be placed on a website, another PR tool is the blog post. It can essentially take the place of the press release with a more modern, approachable presentation for audiences beyond just press, and can serve multiple purposes.

The top reason we use blog posts in PR is to garner links back to a website for SEO purposes. Blog posts can be newsworthy press materials, if they include one of these two elements:

- Industry Trends
- Relevant Stats and Figures

The blog post must be packed full of so much information (with links to cited references) that the press views it as so credible that they must link to the blog post when covering that topic.

We typically handle writing the blog post for the client so that we have control over how it turns out. Then it is posted under a key executive's name on the client's website to build up his or her writing portfolio. Next, we write a short pitch to the press that details the blog post — especially highlighting stats and numbers — mentioning these three things in the close of the pitch:

1. Take any part of this blog post verbatim to quote our client in any story relevant to this topic.

2. Get a fresh take on this topic by interviewing our executive (the "author" of the blog post) for more information.

3. Link to this blog post as a reference in any story you may be working on surrounding this topic.

Blog posts have become an addicting way to do PR because it's providing value on so many levels. Through blog posts, we're providing content for the website which can also turn into social and newsletter content, we're creating a vehicle for earning high-quality links from reputable third-party websites to increase SEO, and of course, as always, we're crushing it through generating killer press coverage.

CHAPTER SIX

WORKING WITH TELEVISION

Mentally putting yourself in the middle of a television station can arm you with the right mindset before pitching this supercharged medium. I have already painted the picture of the typical setting where the news changes in the blink of an eye with continuous deadlines facing the team. Add the pressure of incorporating social and online coverage into the mix, and you're dealing with a proverbial shit-show.

Even amidst newsroom chaos, reporters, producers and news directors manage to remain calm. How? They understand the schedule of their days and you should too.

REGULAR TV NEWS

You've probably noticed there are multiple shows airing at set times throughout the day. These used to be in the straightforward morning and evening hours (starting at 5 p.m. and going into 11 p.m.), but now with news shows creeping into the 11 a.m. and 4 p.m. timeslots, TV news fills the crevices of our days.

While each time-slot displays its own flavor, most feature "regular news," with anchors at their desks in the studio and reporters out in the field. These field reporters go "live on the scene" to provide a visual respite from the studio and more credibility to stories since they are onsite. The greenest reporters are often tasked with the most gruesome reporting jobs — that doesn't mean that they get shocking stories, because that would be exciting. Instead, they are along the side of a mountain freezing in a snowstorm. While the legacy reporters get to talk about it from the comfort of their cushy studio, probably wearing pajama bottoms and fuzzy pink slippers behind the privacy of the studio desk.

Most of the time, PR people aren't trying to get a slot with the anchor (unless there is a place for that; know your show). Rather, they're attempting to get the field reporters to come out and cover their story. PR people will sometimes settle for a "camera," which means that the news sends a camera person, without an actual reporter, to interview your source and shoot some footage, which is delivered to the station and aired later, likely with the anchor "voicing it over" in her fuzzy pink slippers from her perch at the desk.

Timelines and Pitch Tips for General TV News

There is a straight forward system to pitching television news. After following the media etiquette rules, the basis of the script idea and the advice on writing media pitches, success comes down to the most basic of timing details.

If you have must-cover-now news: Send it to the email address designated for the "assignment desk," or general news email, the day before the news occurrence and call the assignment desk to make sure they received it. You can try and ask for the assignment editor, but pretty much whoever answers the "desk" line is acting as the assignment editor that moment. You can mellow out on your verbal pitch here. You're just making sure they received it, accomplishing some of tomorrow's work now, because if it's a feasible story they will "put it in the file" to be discussed tomorrow. Do not call your grandma relaying this "put it in the file" news as your first big PR win. It simply means that it's in the queue to be discussed at their **morning meeting.**

You've secured your spot to be included among the news ideas discussed during the morning meeting, which is held around **9 a.m.** at most television stations. Every station and market is a little different. If the conversation allows, you can ask and make note of the meeting time. (I imagine they all gather around a big table and throw ideas back and forth at each other, with the big boss brusquely vetoing story possibilities with the wave of a thick hand that holds the power to make or break our spotlight aspirations.)

Wait, you're not done. The most important call is yet to be made. You must not leave it to the fates and trust that they will talk about your pitch simply because it is "in the file." **Call on the morning of your desired news coverage day before they go into their 9 a.m. meeting.** You're just making sure your pitch will be discussed in the meeting, but in doing so you might be inadvertently arming the person on the other end of the line with the material they need to talk about your news idea in five to ten seconds flat.

The essence of your call is to remind them that your news opportunity is occurring today. Here is an example of how the dialogue could go.

"This is Amy with the Circus calling about the 12 train cars that will roll into town TODAY. Do you have a second?" I ask in a casual way that holds an undertone of authority, realizing that I'd shortened my introduction line from the pitch I'd used before (Chapter 4) because I have such a unique visual I don't need to say much. The word TODAY is important because it tells them they need to talk about it in the meeting they are about to go into.

"We got it," the frazzled news worker replies.

I know this means they received the pitch and will discuss it in their meeting, so that's all that really needs to be done. But today I've taken a seat in the front row before heading off to glee club. I am in the mood for perfection.

"OK, I just wanted to make sure it's in the file for discussion," I say, explicitly stating what I need. I'm not sure who's on the other end of the line, it could be an intern. "We'll have clowns, lion tamers and live-stock. It should be quite the scene," I coolly further my pitch by paint-ing the visual.

"Yep, it's in the file," she briskly replies.

"Oh great, thank you," I say with what sounds like relief, but I'm just trying to relate on a human level by expressing my own insecurities. Mistaking this for ignorance she feels the need to go on. "That doesn't mean we will cover it. It means we will talk about whether we will cover it or not," she states. "Yup," I reply back with an air of busy authorita-tiveness. Does she think I'm new at this?

For general TV news, it's best to get the morning shift to send cameras out because you'll have a better chance of getting on all the TV sta-tion's news shows, such as the noon news. If you can do a quick "photo op" around 10 a.m. and send the news packing after 10:20 a.m. they will have enough time to get it onto the noon news and possibly repeat the coverage throughout the day (4 p.m. and 5 p.m.) into the evening (10 p.m. and 11 p.m.).

Ten a.m. on weekdays is best for photo ops/press events/press confer-ences. The earlier in the week the better. The closer you get to Friday, the more weekend event competition you'll have.

For An Upcoming Public Event

You do not need to wait to send your information the day before. You might as well send a calendar listing around one week before, in case they air a calendar of events. You can also embark on all of the other fun TV activities: inviting press to come to the event and throwing a pre-event photo op (Chapter 8) to maximize your coverage.

For more on assignment desk pitching, listen to PR Talk podcast episode #39, with Bruce Williams, Assignment Editor at NBC, on **PRtalk.co**

NIGHTTIME NEWS

There is a shift change that sends cameras out in the evening hours, however your chances of getting evening coverage that isn't of the *man-getting-stabbed* variety is greatly reduced during this time. So you'd better have a good reason for not scheduling a separate day-time photo op to promote your nighttime situation. The only reason I could understand is if the event or nighttime news you have going on doesn't really matter. For instance, getting the coverage might help branding efforts later, but it won't help you sell anything the night of.

The nighttime news shift typically comes in around 2 - 3 p.m. They also have news meetings around this time to discuss what the nighttime shift will cover. As you are doing your call-downs you can ask when the nighttime assignment editor arrives and when/if they have their news meeting so that you may determine when to follow up.

MORNING SHOWS

This Golden PR opportunity may be one of the only times you need to plan weeks ahead in TV. When PR people bring up morning shows, most of the time they are talking about the features reporter cutting into the boring news that's occurring back at the station with live segments on fun things. Most of the morning show reporters I've worked with book their own segments, therefore they are the gateway to reams of coverage. When you land a morning show, oftentimes you are landing the chance to hang out with the reporter for the entire morning with live storytelling opportunities about your organization sprinkled throughout.

Pitching Morning Shows

While you might want to start broaching the subject with your morning show reporter about six weeks ahead, the sweet spot to landing stories is around four weeks ahead. Although they all work a little differently. You'll want to assess their typical daily coverage before you start pitching them because your role here is to act like their producer. Not only is acting like a great producer how to secure a "yes" for this particular occurrence, it's how you can win them over for life, gaining frequent bookings. Why wouldn't they continue working with someone who does all the heavy lifting?

Working with Morning Shows

Ideally your pre-pitch research turned up your target's type of coverage — beyond the theme of the coverage and into the semantics: how many segments do they get in a morning and about how long are they? To win them over, you've probably sketched out a brief timeline of the segments you can arrange for them.

Once you get a commitment, ask for their "rundown," which tells you the time and length of each live segment. You need this to book guests. Now start lining up the segments. Some reporters are fine with a few "talking heads," while some will micro-manage your heady tendencies. There is only one way to find out. Run your ideas by them in a brief email, phone call or even text conversation before you start working too hard on prepping and lining people up (this may have already been done in the pitch stage).

You may wonder what to do on live TV if you can't rely on too many talking heads but still need to book guests? The guest might have to partake in an activity while being interviewed, or they could talk while the reporter is doing something active. Think about TV as you may have been told to write — show rather than tell. For example, chefs don't just stand there and talk on TV, they work with the food they are discussing *while* talking about it.

How to turn a "talking head" into a "moving body":

- Have the guest teach the reporter how to do something

- Have the guest demonstrate something while talking about it

- Have the guest tour, show or demonstrate the thing they are talking about

- Have the reporter and guest pitch in to an effort or cause that's being talked about

The general theme here is that the reporter needs to play along in whatever is being discussed. You can also incorporate pictures or visuals into the interview — this relies on the techies back at the station to use what you send ahead of time.

Type up your rundown in order of segments, including:

- The time each segment is slated to go live

- Padding time of when the guest was asked to arrive on-site

  » Always have guests arrive one half hour before their live segment

- Each guest's name, cell phone number and what they will talk about or do on-air

The point of the rundown is to organize yourself and provide it to your team (including the reporter) ahead of time, so it can serve as a replacement for you in case of emergency.

Always paranoid, I run events ahead of time with the thought that if an accident were to prevent me from being there physically, the event would operate smoothly even without me; including prepping each guest. We don't require media training with guests, but we have phone conversations to ensure they are live human beings. We don't overly prep them if they've done "live" TV before. If they are newbies we tone ourselves down and explain that live TV is fun and casual to set them at ease. We casually talk about what they will say/do on-air. Then we causally rattle off these few TV pointers:

- Don't look at the camera. They will stick it in your face and you'll think you are supposed to look at it, but you are supposed to have a conversation with the reporter.

  » If you accidentally glance at the camera, just get over it and move the conversation forward.

- Don't wear white or busy, patterned shirts.

- Turn your cell phone off (remind everyone before the cameras start rolling).

- Relax and smile! Remember, this is fun!

> For more on working with morning show reporters, listen to PR Talk podcast #14, with FOX morning show reporter, Joe V. on **PRtalk.co**

WEEKEND NEWS

Everything I've been telling you in this chapter heavily relies on your work during weekdays (Monday - Friday) during normal working hours (9 a.m. - 5 p.m.). Most shows tend to bulk up their staff at these times too, presenting more opportunities. While getting weekend coverage is very possible, and used to be way too easy, it's harder now due to the budget cuts that traditional media outlets often experience.

Staffs are typically slimmer, not just in the evening, but especially during the weekend.

However, the same timelines and rules that apply during the week loosely apply during the weekend. If you're using a slimmer weekend newsroom staff as an excuse to hit the mall, you're missing out on a prime opportunity. Most of your work will still have been done during the week — you'll have organized your photo op, sent out your pitch, and done an initial round of follow up calls, "making sure they got it."

You are just reserving a little of your time for the weekend by calling again on Saturday to either:

1. **Make sure they know about your weekend event or photo op**, while asking them to send a camera to a weekend occurrence you have. If they do not send a camera, read the next tip.

2. **Make sure they got the footage you submitted to them** from a photo op or event you already put together either during the end of the previous week or earlier that day. Here we are entering a new territory that is shifting the role of the PR professional into more of a media professional.

I'll explain more about how to operate this way in Chapter 8 after running through some additional TV details first.

> For the three top tips for garnering TV news,
> listen to a PR Talk mini-cast on **PRtalk.co**

TELEVISION STAFF TITLES

Titles and roles in television are similar to news radio titles. All the roles I will mention in the radio section relate to TV as well. However, TV stations have more set roles without as much crossover, so it's easier for us to understand. A situation where the assignment editor might also be the news director who might also be the anchor wouldn't necessarily occur in TV like it does in radio, unless it's a very small market.

Here is who you need to know in most large- to medium-sized TV markets:

Assignment Editor

They now sometimes call these people content editors and are getting a little "fancy" with the titles. But, if you just ask for the assignment editor everyone will know what you mean and they might actually think you know what you're talking about if you use this old school language.

This person is going to be your best friend in TV. While they work as a team to decide how they will cover your news, the bulk of the stories go through the assignment editor. Sometimes they will just have the anchor read two sentences of your information on-air and you'd never even know it happened unless you are a shut-in watching all TV stations at once or using a monitoring service. Or they will send a reporter to what you promoted in your PR materials without even telling you. Or you will get a call saying they are 10 minutes away and if your interviewee is three martinis into a power lunch, you haven't planned for the best case scenario. Don't burn bridges. Always prepare for the best and worst case scenarios.

Reporter

You would pitch a reporter directly if they have a specific beat that aligns with your news/subject. For example, if you have a healthcare TV reporter in town and you happen to represent a medical or health subject, you might try this person first because they'll be more invested in getting your news out. Also, coverage by a reporter is better than an assignment editor sending a camera because the reporter may create a more in-depth feature. The reporter might also have a large personal following and will do extra things with the coverage, like posting it to their social channels and nodding to your organization through a link on a blog or a tag on social media.

To clarify, if an assignment editor sends someone out to cover your pitch, it doesn't mean they always send a reporter. Most of the time they send a camera to capture the visual and handle the reporting with an anchor "voice-over." But, it's much better if a reporter comes because they will give the story more time and they are more invested in getting it to actually air. It's easy to throw away 30 seconds of B-roll (general footage without an interview) that took a camera person 15 minutes to shoot, if things get tight in the news line up or the weatherman runs over his allotted time on purpose so he can leave early.

My oldest childhood friend was a TV producer. She told me that an infamous local weatherman would purposely run long during his first weather segment so his last weather segment in the show would get dropped so he could leave early. After awhile she caught on to this and instead of letting him go early, she simply dropped the last 30 seconds of a feel-good story that would typically run at the end. This eventually solved the problem, and the weatherman resumed carrying his load of the work.

Producer

The producer pieces the entire show together from behind the scenes; arranging the interviews, putting the segments in order and more. In some cases, you would pitch the producer especially if there isn't an assignment editor, like with an entertainment-focused show. But, on typical straight-forward news shows in local markets you'll rely on the assignment editor, and the producer simply puts it all together. You might try and find out who is producing special shows at odd times and see if they are the decision-maker.

Digital Producer

Just like in print, the digital producer takes all of the station's stories and gets them up on the website or social media. Not all stories that air on

TV make it online, just as not all online stories make it on TV. In some instances, the later concept works out just great, especially if you are after SEO results. If you're in the business of garnering SEO, this person, not the assignment editor, might be your best friend!

For more from a digital producer, listen to PR Talk podcast episode #31 with Greg Retsinas, head of digital for TEGNA on **PRtalk.co**

CHAPTER SEVEN

WORKING WITH RADIO & PODCASTS

Radio just really drives me crazy. I have perfected the radio timelines for general news shows down to such a science that it can sometimes bite me in the ass.

REGULAR RADIO NEWS

Getting coverage on radio stations that focus on news all the time is a little easier than breaking onto a pop radio station for coverage during the brief moments when they aren't playing music or spreading celebrity gossip. For the regular news radio stations, which could be on FM or AM frequency or even SiriusXM, you want to focus your work around drive times, ideally the morning drive time — 6 a.m. to 9 a.m.

Timelines for Regular Radio News

Send your news about one day ahead, but realize you'll have to call to pitch your story the morning you want your interview to run. Don't call during drive time. Most stations will have time to talk with you if you call right after drive time. Give them only about 5 - 10 minutes to breathe after drive time ends at 9 a.m. Wait much longer than five minutes and you're running the risk of bumping into their morning meeting (if they have one) or breaking into shift change.

Pitch Tips for Regular Radio News

You definitely want to catch the person in charge when calling. The person with the news director title is also often the main reporter that's on-air during the shift. If you call the station's newsroom phone number at the right time, you'll most likely get the person in charge. Do not call the receptionist. If that's the only number, ask to be transferred to the newsroom and make a note of the newsroom number for future use.

Radio Pitch Caveats

Here is how calling at just the right time and following some of the earlier script suggestions can bite you in the ass. You need to be ready for success. Immediately. If the person in charge on the other end of the pitch likes what you have to say, they very well might want to interview someone right away. This is done through phone interviews, affectionately coined "phoners" by people in the biz.

If you add an undertone of authoritative urgency to your voice, and relatively sound like you know what you are talking about, they might actually want to interview YOU right then and there. This is how you can get into trouble. If you don't already have clearance from your client or boss, you cannot do the interview. You must punt the interview to someone else, which is ideal if you are working for multiple clients because anyone working in-house on the client side will have much more information than you do. Have your client ready and willing to do the interview at a moment's notice when you know you'll be proactively pitching radio.

If radio calls you for an interview you didn't pitch, that's another story, but it's very irritating to anyone who works in radio to be proactively pitched something that cannot be delivered ASAP.

Another scenario is with an event (10 a.m. photo op). Pitch radio to see if they can attend. If not, they can possibly catch up with your interviewee after the event for a phoner, like around 2 p.m., which is another dead zone (free time) for radio. However, you'll be dealing with a shift change so you may have to re-pitch, re-committing another press contact to the story.

RADIO MORNING SHOWS & SPECIAL SEGMENTS

When you are riding in your car with the drop top down…listening to…wait for it…news radio…(never knew adulthood could be so sexy)…you'll notice the difference between straight up news — when the news of the day is relayed in quick moments in time — and feature stories — longer segments that require more care and planning. Many news radio stations will air both types of stories, but the stations that have more variety to them — being mostly FM music radio stations that mix thoughtful news coverage or what's happening around town into their drive time routine — will be of the long-lead feature story variety.

Timelines for Radio Morning Shows and Special Segments

To get onto these special types of shows or segments, I always think that approaching them three weeks ahead is the golden rule, however you'd probably still be alright with two weeks ahead. Even if you send the pitch three weeks ahead, you'll still have to follow up two weeks ahead, and possibly again at one week ahead.

RADIO STAFF TITLES

Titles depend on what type of station or show you are pitching. There's popular radio, typically on FM frequency, and news radio on both AM and FM frequency. Let's dig into the fun stuff first.

FM or Entertainment Radio

The people working on music radio stations aren't sitting in news meetings deciding what fire they are going to report on or what ambulance they are going to chase. However, you've probably noticed that some stations incorporate current events into their repertoire, especially during morning drive time. Depending on the listenership, some stations are going to be more serious than others.

That's not to say one style is better than the other because it depends on what you are pitching. Pitching a music or entertainment event will have an easier time getting picked up on entertainment radio stations. PR topics that aren't very entertaining are going to have a harder time getting on entertainment-based stations. But, it still might be worth looking at stations that spend time on stories beyond the entertainment variety.

Here's who you need to know:

Host/DJ (Anchor)

The DJ or host/anchor is the on-air voice, but in the instance of a smaller radio station, they might also be the news director, deciding what stories to mention on-air during their show. As advertising dollars move online, budget cuts mean that many stations don't have the luxury of hiring different roles. Therefore, the hosts must do it all. Luckily, many times there are two sharing the heavy morning show burden together.

Moreover, interviews are getting shorter, if they are happening at all. Two popular morning show hosts in Portland, Ore. that I interviewed on PR Talk (find at PRtalk.co) drove home the point that radio show hosts only have eight seconds to grab listeners. Listeners will change the station if they tune into the middle of an interview and don't immediately grasp what's being discussed. Popular radio shows combat that short window by axing the entire concept of the interview. That's not to say that your news won't be shared. The hosts may just share it in a shorter amount of time without interviewing anyone.

It becomes clear how shorter interviews (or none at all) could eliminate some of the producer and news director roles. I imagine hosts like these scan news sources (including their inbox flooded with PR pitches), select what they want to highlight and simply talk about it in the space of time that the rest of their show will allow. There is no need to schedule interviews or organize with PR people. They might be using your PR materials, like your expertly crafted pitch, without you ever knowing it. However, here's how some of the other roles come into play.

Promotion Director

If you want to creatively align with a radio station, contact this person and work out ideas like offering giveaways and freebies as part of an on-air contest that gets your brand's name out there with frequency.

Program Director

If you're pitching music, shoot your pitch over to this person.

News Radio Shows (FM or AM)

Here's where more PR opportunities lie. The newsrooms for these types of stations operate like television newsrooms. Assignment desks not only receive pitches and tips, but also monitor news sources through tools like police scanners (a constant feed of what police are discussing out in the field, such as emergencies and crimes) and Twitter. While there are straight-forward roles, the person answering the assignment desk phone might also be the on-air personality that reports on the story you've just sent over.

Here are the roles you're likely to encounter:

Assignment Editor/News Director

Not only do they work the assignment desk — which includes answering calls from PR enthusiasts like us, along with staying on top of what's going on in the world — they also assign the stories to specific reporters. Sometimes this role would be called the news director in radio.

Field Reporter

That's not to say that reporters can't pitch their own stories for inclusion in the day's coverage, convincing their team that a particular story needs to be told. The field reporter in comparison to the anchor is that lucky person who gets to stand in four feet of snow in the middle of a raging blizzard telling everyone it's snowing when all we need to do is look outside. But for the most part it is exciting work that keeps them on the go all day long. The work, however, can be emotionally draining, incorporating an air of danger. Perhaps this is why after a time they aim to get promoted to anchor.

Anchor/Radio Host

The anchor rarely leaves the studio during the course of their shift. They serve as a sort of emcee to the entire show, bridging the content together. They're probably "voicing over" (explaining without an interview) stories in addition to tossing to field reporters. You would rarely pitch an anchor as they are driving the entire ship. However, in radio the anchor might also be the field reporter, which might also very well be the news director.

PODCASTS: THE NEW RADIO

Podcasting has become all the rage. There are almost too many of them to weed through and the media database services are just playing catch up. However, you could think of podcasts as the new radio. Podcasts can range from having a ton of listeners to being someone's pet-project who's only listener is their grandma.

Both are fine to pitch especially if you think about how a small podcast can provide an opportunity for your spokesperson to practice. Being interviewed in a non-visual format can be challenging because, unless a video component is incorporated, it's void of the visual queues that we rely on to communicate. Also, news radio interviews tend to be short and abrupt, mirroring the personalities of some radio anchors, therefore the intimidation factor can be huge. Whereas, the podcasting format is longer and more conversational, therefore providing a nice "warm up" to more intimidating forms of news and press personalities.

Also many businesses want to jump on the podcasting bandwagon and start their own without having any information or experience. Getting interviewed on podcasts first can be a great introduction to the podcasting process for those interested in starting one.

Another benefit to doing podcast interviews is the SEO factor. Many podcasts have websites where a blog post, or "show notes," will be uploaded in conjunction with the podcast episode. Those sites are great places to obtain links back to your website after doing an interview.

Discovering Podcasts to Pitch

Just like any other media list, you have to decide which parameters you want to put around potential podcasts to pitch. There are over one million podcasts* covering hundreds, if not thousands, of topics. And guess what, they take guest requests in different ways. Some have a formal process, while a simple email pitch will do for others. Of course, there are the professional media podcasts that could be pitched the same way you would pitch radio, TV or even print. Not all podcasts even have guests, so you want to eliminate those right away. If they do have guests, do you (or your client) fit their criteria?

Once you have narrowed your hit list based on the above guidelines, now you can start to look at stats and data to make informed decisions about your target podcasts. At least that is the idea.

Since podcasting is a relatively new medium, the stats and figures are not in one place. In fact, podcasters and marketers can't even agree on what is important to weigh when figuring out which podcasts to pitch, much less actually getting the stats we need.

---

* https://mypodcastreviews.com/podcast-industry-statistics/

So, we have to hack it a bit. First, you have to decide what stats you are going to compare. A few good indicators to start with are:

- Reach (downloads and listens)

- Frequency of episodes (daily, weekly, monthly, random)

- Age of podcast (how long it has been around)

- Total number of episodes*

- Domain authority of the podcast website

- Number of Apple Podcasts ratings (as well as number of stars)

- Number of Apple Podcasts reviews (including sentiment)

- Apple Podcasts popularity (0-25, but only relative to other similar Apple Podcasts podcasts)

- SoundCloud (or other apps/platform) followers

If a goal of your PR and or podcast appearances is SEO, you can factor in the link opportunities, social reach and other content creation angles.

Of course, if you aren't hitting the correct audience or don't have the right guest to pitch, none of the stats matter. So you need to also catalog the categories of the potential podcasts to pitch.

We start with finding the relevant podcasts, creating a spreadsheet and then adding the stats we find from a variety of sources. Starting with a good old fashioned Google search can be the way to go. Then plug in the podcasts and add the stats you find. You may not be able to find all the stats for each podcast, but since they should all be in Apple Podcasts (and if not, you probably don't want to pitch it anyway) you can go heavy on using Apple metrics.

---

* Note, be sure that the podcast is still recording new episodes. We are guilty of identifying what seemed like a solid guest opportunity to then notice they haven't released a new episode since 2017…

Finally, once you have the data inputted into your spreadsheet, assign a subjective 1 - 5 priority score for all your potential podcast targets and pitch accordingly.

You can also subscribe to a few email lists, such as PodcastGuests.com, that send out weekly requests from podcasts looking for guests.

Media Podcasts

Now of course most media with any presence at all are creating podcasts, making you wonder if this is another new "traditional" media category to pitch or just another fad. I would say that for the most part it's best to just stick with pitching traditional media categories first. So if you want to get in your daily newspaper, just pitch the appropriate reporter at your daily newspaper, not the podcast. And if the paper recognizes how the resulting coverage could be expanded upon in the podcast, they might then funnel you into the podcast.

Many media podcasts are side projects by the media that eventually fizzle out. Moreover, they feature reporters and editors talking to each other and not even interviewing outside sources.

But, if you have something unique or intriguing, it might be worth perusing your key media's podcast lineup to see if something fits. Your story might be better suited for a special podcast put out by the media outlet rather than running it directly with that media outlet. For example, one of our city's top radio stations has a podcast called "Talking Trash," which covers sustainability. The radio station itself plays music for the most part with the morning show anchors bantering back and forth about the news of the day, leaving little room for outside interviews. Therefore, getting a sustainability client or project on the Talking Trash podcast might be a great way to still reach the radio station's listeners — and more importantly perhaps garner a link from a reputable media website.

How to Pitch Podcasts

Now that you have identified your podcast hit list, the process for pitching an appearance can be very similar to other pitches. The more you know about your target (which could be the host, producer, or someone else with the organization) the better pitch you can put together.

You will have to start with identifying and building up your pitching assets which can include:

- A short pitch on why you/they will be a great guest

- One-sheet about your guest, including: short bio, topics they can discuss, potential questions they can answer, headshot or image to use

- Potentially how you/they will promote the appearance

- Links to past appearances (with comparative stats if that helps)

- A website landing page with all of the above information is helpful

CHAPTER EIGHT

OPERATING LIKE A NEWSROOM

Where there is action there is news to be created. Examples include a group volunteering outside, a large event being set up, or a gallery installation. Many people call these types of situations "photo ops," which is short for photo opportunity.

Photo ops can get you a lot of juice and they don't always require press releases as long as they are captured visually. For example, if a team is already volunteering in the community, have someone take a picture of the action. You can then send that picture to the local newspaper, online business section, or appropriate trade publication.

While pictures are a must in documenting this type of effort, media advisories (Chapter 3) can help you invite media to cover your photo op. On a slow news day, you could even luck out with getting TV coverage. Even though you are taking photos as back up, it's best if reporters and photographers come to you and take their own photos because there's a higher probability they'll use them.

However, we do not live in a perfect world and sometimes breaking news prevents the media from attending. When all else fails, pull out your mobile phone and shoot any of the press event ideas that follow.

PRESS EVENTS: PHOTOS & VIDEO OPPORTUNITIES

Don't have a cartload of crazy clowns moving into town to promote your thing? Here are some other ideas:

- Groundbreaking for new construction

- Ribbon cutting for new office/location*

- Oversized check presentation

- Public art unveiling

- Art installation

- Exhibitors moving into a tradeshow

- Large scale event set up/move-in

- Special performance for children (children cannot be photographed without their guardian signing a photo disclaimer)

- The measuring of a race course (run, walk or bike event)

- New building/structure tours

- Moving days for notable organizations

- Volunteering or doing something active in the community

- Large-scale donation of food, clothing or other physical item *drop off*

---

* Add more to it: incorporate other important things. Talking heads — such as politicians, VIPs, donors — talking about important things are good but visually thin. What can your photo op players literally DO during their 20 minutes of fame?

- The event itself (along with or instead of a pre-event photo op) — don't forget the event you've been hired to promote is a photo op in and of itself

- Any other thing you can make visual or active

TV newsrooms appreciate this type of proactivity, especially during the weekend when there is likely only one camera person working. Getting one or two news crews out to your event is great, but why not place your story on all the stations? Follow up with the missing parties by sending them the photos and video you've taken yourself. Here's how:

TIMELINES ON SENDING PHOTOS/VIDEO TO TV

Send your footage and photos by 2 p.m. to the assignment desks on the day the photo op occurred, during weekdays or weekends, and then call right away to make sure they received your email. If they didn't receive your email, keep sending and following up until you are sure they received your materials. **You must send this by 2 p.m. otherwise you will bump against their 5 p.m. news shows.**

Most news stations air 5 p.m. shows, so operate in a timely manner to get on that show. If you make it onto "the 5 p.m." the story will likely run again on that station's following evening news shows and maybe into the next day's early morning shows.

Enlist a monitoring service to inform you which stations run your coverage. If your photo op was during the middle of the weekday and the monitoring service shows it didn't run that evening, your opportunity to get it to run the following day is probably shot.

Unless your photo op was on a Friday. While it might be hard for press to attend a Friday photo op, Saturday's weekend shift presents a prime opportunity to run Friday's footage. As far as press outreach, follow all the same material delivery and follow up steps on Friday, but then call the stations that didn't run your story on Saturday morning. Likewise, if your photo op occurred on Saturday, follow all the same steps on Saturday, but then call the stations that didn't run it on Sunday morning.

A new crew may be working on the weekends, so you aren't being too obnoxious in continuing to call. Unless you're getting the feeling you are being obnoxious — read the room. If it's a new crew you're simply repeating some of these steps again. Calling to make sure they:

A) Know about the photo op that just occurred

B) Make sure they received the video/photos

If you're feeling uncomfortable, just play dumb, saying you're unsure if they ran it, so you're resending the information. You might actually get a great update that it ran and you no longer need to annoy that station.

And finally, stop calling the station if you get a no. Do not attempt to convince another contact at the station. **No means no.**

———

To garner print (online) coverage, also send your photos the day of the event or the very next day. While you may not have to be as timely for print (depending on the news topic), you might as well play it safe.

TAKING PHOTOS FOR THE MEDIA

Most of us have a camera in our pocket or purse, which is good enough if you follow some basic rules. Here are my tips for taking pictures with your smartphone or any other camera when hiring a pro isn't an option:

1. Be aware of your lighting. Shooting outside or near natural light (big windows) is ideal, but be aware of the sun's

location. You don't want the sun directly in front of you or even right behind your subject.

2. Depending on the type of phone camera, you may have better luck zooming by walking closer to your subject to snap the shot, or simply take the photo from afar and then zoom in during editing. Many phones (including iPhones) lose photo quality by manually zooming on your phone.

3. Use the "exposure lock" feature on an iPhone (and most other smartphones).

    a. This is done by touching your screen to "lock" in on your subject so the camera will focus on what you want it to, not constantly refocusing itself on some random dude in the background.

    b. In hurrying to capture a live moment (as opposed to a setup shot), simply tap the screen on the subject you want to be in focus.

4. Most of the time a horizontal photo is best, so turn that phone sideways, except vertical photos work better for Instagram. You can't win!

5. Turn the "LIVE" feature off.

6. If you need a high resolution photo, use the "HDR" setting. See more tips below about resolution.

7. Try shooting from different perspectives. If you have time, crouch down and get another angle, shoot from the hip (literally) or find some high ground to capture a scene.

8. Don't forget about the client or partners. Do you want to get the logo on the shirt they're wearing or the banner that just happens to be in the background? Be intentional, but not obvious.

More On Resolution

I don't have the perfect answer to what it means when a reporter asks for a "high resolution" image. It gets pretty complicated and varies depending on what they are actually using the image for. For example, the desired resolution is different for a print magazine compared to an online guest blog post, but here is a guide:

Pixels are more important than file size, however, your image is likely large enough if it is 500 KB or more, unless it is for a glossy magazine or a billboard.

3,000 pixels wide is probably good enough for any outlet. By default most iPhones will take an image at 72 DPI (dots per inch), but if it is big enough (by number of pixels) it will translate into a smaller (by actual print size, inches or centimeters) image. Typically the term DPI is used for printing, but it can be edited in Photoshop or other image editing software. When in doubt for a glossy, leave the file size big. You may have to share via Dropbox or Google Drive.

Sending Photos to Press

If you only have a few photos that aren't too big in resolution, go ahead and just attach them in your email message. Five MB would be too big to send to any media contact, unless they are a glossy magazine that has asked for the large image, and in that case you may need to share via Dropbox, Google Drive or a file sharing app. Be sure to provide "suggested photo captions" (see Chapter 3) in the body of your message and label each photo accordingly.

If you have a lot of photos, send them because TV loves visuals! However, don't overload them with junky photos. Delete unusable photos to save your press friends some time. An abundance of photos should always be submitted via Dropbox, Google Drive, or another file sharing service.

VIDEO INSIGHTS

RULE #1: There are no rules. Just take the damn video. Perfection is the greatest hindrance of all. Since nothing is ever perfect, taking the perfect video would be impossible. Plus, TV has followed the lead of the consumers who are used to the fluid, imperfect style of social media and reality TV shows, not to mention everyone's experience working and reporting from home during the COVID-19 pandemic. Today we gravitate toward imperfection as an interpretation of authenticity.

Just follow these simple tips when taking video:

- Be aware of your lighting and shooting angles
- Use exposure lock
- Do not zoom with camera zoom, get closer to your subject or zoom in during editing
- Shoot horizontally (might also shoot a vertical Instagram option)
- Use a tripod to keep steady
- Use a microphone (lavaliere mic for $15 on Amazon)
- Think about how you will download, store and share your videos, as file size can be very large

If you can't do any of the above, don't worry about it and just hit the video button on your phone and see what happens.

Once you have your video and photos, you're going to have to muster up some tenacity throughout the follow-up process.

Sending Videos to Press

Attachments that are too big won't even arrive into in-boxes. So if it's a big video, I'd probably send it via Dropbox, Hightail, WeTransfer or create a YouTube account. Upload your video(s) and make sure they can be downloaded by others.

Make it easy for the media by using a platform everyone's comfortable with since you don't know who is being tasked with downloading your materials and what their comfort level is with various platforms. Keep it simple.

Use all the skills you've learned in previous sections to follow-up on videos, probably simultaneously while following-up on something else like a photo or press release.

PRESS CONFERENCES

Have something important to say? Then by all means hold a press conference, right? Wrong. Press conferences should only be held for matters that greatly affect the public. Announcing news of important public concern is the only time you can highlight talking heads without other things happening and expect the press to show up.

Timing the Press Conference

Your news better be pretty important if you have the audacity to hold a press conference. That's why it can occur at a time that's convenient for your team. But, if you are leading communication for an important situation, you probably want a lot of people to know what you have to say. Therefore you'd hold your conference at the time that could hit most news shows: not in the afternoon to avoid bumping up against evening news deadlines.

Situations Calling for Press Conferences:

- Natural disasters — your response, instructions or updates

- Public safety matters — your response, instructions or updates

- Public health matters — your response, instructions or updates

- Updates on major crimes or news people might be following

- Announcements on changes in public office or policy

The best time to hold any press event, including press conferences and photo ops, is roughly 10 a.m. during the weekdays, or right after the morning meeting held at most newsrooms, which is around 9 a.m. during the weekdays.

> For more on how to operate like a newsroom,
> listen to a PR Talk mini-cast episode on **PRtalk.co**

CHAPTER NINE

PR CHEATS

The bulk of this book has focused on painstaking customization and care when approaching the media. By now you might be wondering if there is a faster, more efficient way to do PR. Absolutely, yes; under these two conditions:

1. The information is very newsworthy

2. You don't have enough time or budget

Often with pieces that are very newsworthy, there is limited time because you're running up against the expiration clock of news. Therefore, a simple pitch — possibly linking to a blog post with more information or to get links for SEO — sent to a large number of *appropriate* news contacts could work.

Shotgunning Your Approach

You can build vast lists through a media database and just go about it the more simple way, which is to pick the beat(s) that would attract a reporter to the story, along with ideal locations and medium type. If you fear you'll get too many queries to manage — when practicing the shotgun approach, it should probably be for a story that's attractive enough to actually warrant such fear — the database should allow further segmentation based on demographics like audience size, designated market area (DMA), reach and language.

You may be able to email the pitch to everyone on your list through your media database software, making it that much more efficient. If you take that approach, pay special attention to targets that take (or do not take) specific actions (opened the email, clicked on a link, etc.) and follow-up accordingly.

The PR maximizer still takes time to separate the list by media category, or other criteria, and spends as little as 15 minutes slightly modifying the pitch to fit each category. They also consider timing nuances: releasing the pitch at appropriate times of day depending on the medium or the show timing for broadcast.

Ideally, you still have a little budget or time left to quickly research the hardest targets' work. Adjust your pitch to align with their recent work covering the newsworthy topic. Besides complimenting the reporter by indicating that you've noticed their work, your pitch should serve as a way to fit into their ongoing coverage of the topic, thus helping them out.

If time is of the essence or your pitch is so successful, the remaining budget can be spent coordinating interviews or handling other media requests.

PRESS RELEASE
DISTRIBUTION SERVICES

While we're talking about shortcuts, let's address the idea of disseminating press releases through PR distribution services, sometimes mistakenly called, "the wire." Potential clients still ask us about this method and some PR people still think it's a viable option.

Promoting a direct feed into the inboxes of thousands of journalists, the cost of PR distribution services range from in the thousands all the way down to free. Since newsrooms subscribe to receive press releases from *some* of the services, an incorrect illusion that guaranteed press release pick up remains. The promise is enticing because it would eliminate the list building and media research process, along with our follow-up procedures and the uncertainty of sending something out with nothing to show for it.

After releasing on the paid services you'll immediately receive impressive reports outlining where your news went with fancy graphs and charts detailing the interaction with the release. And then the coverage starts to quickly follow, with a list of hits ranging from notable media outlets to the obscure, no matter what type of story you've sent.

The Hits Are Like Shell Companies

If something seems too good to be true, it probably is. A cynic like me will follow these stories back to the original source, which essentially can't be found. In most instances, while the hit appears to be on the dream publication's website, try to click backward through the website to see where it lives on the website, and the story is nowhere. Or go in the opposite direction, through the outlet's homepage, search for the hit, and it will not be found.

These services must have reciprocal media agreements, creating fake, unsearchable areas on media websites for most "wire" news. Like a graveyard. Believe me, I really wish the hits were real. It would make our jobs so much easier and the clients are always extremely impressed and happy with the reports. It's hard to tell them that the fee didn't amount to anything because the hits are fake. Actually, I have a hard time believing that something, especially connected to the media, would be so deceitful.

Google Steps in For Policing

But, you might hear that distribution services generate links to websites.

In fact, this used to be true. However, as people began to overuse this benefit, Google quickly caught on. Since just blindly throwing a release on the wire for the sake of a link is in direct opposition with Google's mission to serve up high-authority information, Google began penalizing websites that used such services.

Customers of services that gave links out, like PR Web, would be penalized in the form of decreased website authority. Therefore, using these services ended up *hurting* their SEO, which was Google's way of decreasing the overuse. Once people caught on, Google removed the penalty, but now links from sites like PR Web aren't worth anything for SEO because the links are tagged as "nofollow," which tells Googlebot not to count them. So, if you have a client pay the $250 entry fee for each release, you aren't giving them good counsel.

There's Always a Catch-22

However, you must have learned by now that nothing is straightforward in PR. Annoyingly, there are some instances where using a PR distribution service is not just beneficial, but part of long-standing custom.

The reputable distribution services are beneficial when your news is very powerful or from a famous entity. Newsroom staff do monitor the more higher-end services, so if something important comes through, they will put it in its proper place, for example not hidden in an unsearchable page on their website. Therefore, these services can save you a lot of time.

When news is released from a public company, it's customary to also use a reputable distribution service to ensure compliance with regulatory requirements that demand their news is made public. While PR professionals could create comprehensive lists through media software, many err on the side of caution and use the service — probably along with their own custom lists — if they are full PR maximizers.

Distribution Services Compared

If you are doubting me, review a Veracity blog post on PRtalk.co that goes into this in exhausting detail with real examples. Many of the services are outlined at the bottom of the post, differentiating between price and other details. But, I can simply tell you that the best services are the most expensive services. When investing in a wire service, or advising your clients to, make sure its worth everyone's while.

PR Newswire seems to be the most effective with national ($825+), regional ($475+) and statewide ($355+) pricing.* Specific targets, such as multicultural, Native American, African American, Hispanic markets and more, can be added. Even if the story isn't knocking anyone's socks off, you still could get a few real *non-shell-company* hits off it.

We haven't used BusinessWire, but it doesn't have the worst reputation either. With a set-up fee you can target specific cities ($210+), states ($225+), regions ($250+) and the nation ($675), as well as global ($3,725+)* and specific international regions such as North America, Latin America and Asia-Pacific.

THE "WIRE"

The Wire is like one of these PR distribution services, but for journalists. Stories running on wires like the Associated Press (AP) or Reuters are syndicated — meaning a media outlet can republish one of the syndicated stories rather than assigning a reporter to cover it.

PR people should approach wire services just like they would approach any outlet or media contact, but perhaps with even more finesse. Landing a story with a wire reporter is huge because it could mean multiple stories either on the local (for example the AP used to have a Portland branch), regional, national or international level.

---

* These prices were as of February of 2020, and may have changed.

OTHER PR SHORTCUTS

There are countless other tools that today's PR pros use for research, media relations, social media and education. Here are a few of the tools I keep close by on my PR Cheatsheet:

HARO

Most PR folks have heard about HARO, which stands for Help A Reporter Out. You can sign up to receive emails for press opportunities. We believe the value of HARO has declined over the past few years and good PR opportunities remain elusive. If you sign up for an account, err on the side of caution and really narrow in on what you want to receive when selecting the requests you'll receive. Once you start to receive the emails, you can create your own criteria on when to respond, detailed on a blog post by Veracity, at PRtalk.co.

Google Alerts and/or Talkwalker

Once you start to generate media coverage, you'll need to know when stories run. In a perfect world, reporters would let us know every time we're included in a story, but again, nothing is ever perfect. If you have the budget, use a high-quality media tracking company like Cision or Critical Mention.

With or without the budget for this service, you should also set up free Google Alerts for key branded terms, top executives and products/services. This free tool sends email notifications when your tracked terms are detected. Talkwalker is another monitoring tool (with a free version) that also tracks mentions in news platforms, blogs, forums, websites and Twitter.

MOZ

If SEO is a PR goal, use the MozBar browser extension in Chrome to see the Domain Authority of any website as a consideration metric before pitching it. Moz also provides other SEO tools for SEO PR efforts. You can create a free account to use the MozBar extension. (SEO PR is covered extensively in Chapter 10).

Cision, Meltwater, Agility PR Solutions, Muck Rack, SparkToro

Most likely you'll want to subscribe to some sort of media database, monitoring, outreach and/or reporting software. They each have their pros and cons, with different price points. I suggest investing some real time into deciding which tool(s) is right for you and your organization, unless that decision has already been made, then invest that time in learning to be efficient with the selected software.

Awardzee

Awardzee is a free searchable database of more than 5,000 business awards. A great place to get started or round out your awards submission research.

What National Day Is It?

There are several websites that feature various "national days," including: National Day Calendar, National Day Today, What National Day Is It? and National Day Archives. Peruse one of these and create your own calendar for the relevant days and/or add them to your overall content calendar.

PR Talk Podcast

Want to know how to pitch a local TV station, vertical trade magazine or understand more about the PR research process? I have recorded more than 100 episodes of the PR Talk Podcast (PRtalk.co) with expert advice and how-to's just for you.

> All of the services mentioned
> above are linked on **PRtalk.co**

CHAPTER TEN

INFUSING OTHER DISCIPLINES

Rarely have I mentioned other marketing disciplines like social media, content marketing, search engine marketing (SEO), and advertising. But they all fit together. In fact, PR can be used as a way to inform the other marketing disciplines.

The messaging you dig into as you uncover not only your organization's goals but also the motivations and desires of your audiences can help create impactful copy for websites, advertising and more. It can also be converted into what's used as the keyword and search terms for SEO.

The topics within your PR timeline can easily be converted into social and content posts. For example, a press release can transform into a blog post for your website, which should ideally get about three separate social media posts directing people back to your website.

The sales department can also use your PR work. Materials such as fact sheets, press releases and press kits can be converted into sales collateral. Some of it can even be used verbatim as a leave-behind, in a pinch.

In many cases, your talking points around both general organizational themes and messaging surrounding high-stakes changes and issues can be used by multiple departments, from sales and marketing to management and training.

And lastly, any PR coverage generated should be shared with sales teams to follow up with new business leads or keep in touch with current customers. Your hard earned PR coverage is also great fodder for email marketing.

SEO PR: THE NEW FRONTIER

"The hard links to get." Matt Cutts, Google's former head of web spam was referencing PR coverage as he talked about how to increase a website's Search Engine Optimization (SEO) — meaning how to get websites to rank higher in the search engines.

The Three Top Ways to Increase SEO:

1. How the site is built: Make sure someone builds it SEO friendly. Do a little research because once it's done you can't go back and fix it without spending more money.

2. Frequent and consistent content: Create a lot of content (blogging) on your website, then market it through social media and more to drive users to your site.

3. Garner links to your website from other sites: Get other websites to write about you and in doing so they'll hopefully link to your website.

Savvy SEO people constantly seek external links to get websites to rank higher in the competitive territory of the world-wide-web. Many SEO professionals are reaching out to website managers across the world to either get links or fix suboptimal links.

It's true that they aren't spinning press releases or reaching out with pitches, but it doesn't matter. Link building is a different form of PR.

Not only will organizations pay a hefty fee for increased search rankings, sometimes it's their only PR purpose. This makes sense for those relying on their online presence to bring in revenue, like ecommerce businesses. But, even if you are a lead generation site or rely solely on referrals, the authority that comes with third-party accreditation from a high Google rank provides tremendous value.

SEO PR Basics

Before getting into the more technical SEO PR details, let's start with the basics. Be sure to include the link you want your target to include in any online coverage in all pitches and press releases. Sometimes journalists will copy and paste directly from your materials, so there's a better chance they'll include the link in their coverage if it's already in your materials.

Not All Websites Are Created Equal

For the most part, just doing some general PR will increase SEO because most traditional press will include news on their website if the news has already been placed within their traditional medium. If they don't, one must wonder if that outlet is worth pitching.

But, if SEO truly is a concern, you need to go beyond the typical PR steps and examine websites of the outlets you're pitching or just pitch websites and blogs directly. There is no true social climber like SEO. Some websites, especially reputable press sites, will bring more street cred to your website.

Add a column that tracks the clout of each website to your media lists. Here's what to look for:

- Does the outlet even have a website?
- Do they offer links?
  - » They probably won't provide a policy around links,

even if they have a policy. That's why someone will
need to research if/how they typically link in a story.

- Are the links "follow" links?

  » "Follow" links are better than "nofollow" links because
  "nofollow" links specifically tell search engines to with-
  hold the full value of the link, often because it is from a
  paid advertisement or sponsorship.

- How reputable is the website according to Google?

  » While Google will not specifically tell you how reputable it thinks your site is, there are third party measuring tools that can give you an idea of how you stack up,
  especially against your competitors.

Google ranks the pages of websites, considering some more reputable
than others, thus bringing them up in searches, therefore driving more
traffic to higher ranked sites. While the big media players, like the *New
York Times,* are highly-ranked, you'd be surprised that the smaller community papers' websites are also pretty well-ranked because they are
also media. Google loves media!

How to Track a Website's Google Reputation

Tracking the website's Domain Authority (DA) is the best way to
understand how reputable Google thinks the website is. A free DA
tracking tool we love is Moz. If you have Chrome and sign into Moz
each day there is a toolbar that brings up the DA of any website you
are on. You can quickly vet opportunities this way, deciding where to
spend your time.

Extra Work Required to Get Yummy Links

While getting standard old PR will likely increase your search rankings
automatically, it might behoove some of you to go the extra mile in
adding search results as a goal of the PR. If you decide to go this route,

your actions in earning links will depend on the type of medium you're working with.

Television

Many larger-market TV stations employ digital editors or producers that decide which on-air stories will also end up online. To make the cut, your story probably needs to grab the attention of a reporter since 30 seconds of straight B-roll captured from a camera person probably won't work. Getting a reporter to cover you, rather than just a camera person, is always the best case scenario anyway. Not only will you get a longer, more in-depth story, the reporter might also broaden the story's reach by posting it to their social channels.

Now, if all you're after is the link, why go to the trouble of getting a TV reporter to cover you? Sometimes all the digital editor/producer needs is content, so they also look for stories to post online, and consequently share on social, that haven't graced TV. But they won't run any old story. It probably needs to relate to the local market — like an event that people actually want to attend or a cause that people might care about.

Radio

Don't even go there. I'm sorry, we're just not seeing the point. We're not seeing the radio interviews we land ending up online. Have I mentioned that I'm kinda over it? If you are interested in SEO, review the podcast section as podcast interviews are easier ways to earn links.

Print

I've mentioned that many times what you land in print will also end up online. Sometimes you don't even need to take any extra steps assuming the links are in your pitch, especially with smaller outlets. But just like with TV, there are also digital editors/producers. Pitch them if you're sick of getting newspaper ink on your fingertips.

Social Media

Most media outlets are also very active on social media. While according to Google, links from sites like Facebook, Twitter and LinkedIn do not really count as unique links to your site, they certainly send social signals to the search algorithms telling them that your site and content is relevant and worthwhile.

Also, pseudo social media sites like Quora and Reddit may be a good place to share your news.

Blogs and Straight Up Websites

A website or blog doesn't have to be associated with a media outlet to have SEO PR value. If your target market is interested in the site's topic or the site is relevant to your industry, it very well may be a great place to get some PR coverage and links. Industry blogs and newsletters, review sites, and even government and university websites could be included in your media lists.

Other Ways to Be Strong at SEO PR

If you've gotten online press coverage in the past and they didn't include a link, go back to the contact and ask them to slap a link into the article. If you think asking your press contact for the link would be annoying, ask the digital editor or webmaster for the link. Be specific about where you want the link and what you think it should link to.

Use a tool like Moz Link Explorer, SEMrush Backlink Analytics or Ahrefs to assess past coverage (there are free or trial versions to start). Analyze past coverage to determine:

- If the coverage links to your website. If it doesn't, ask the outlet's webmaster/digital editor to retroactively add it.

- Check to see that the links you have are "follow" links. If you have any "nofollow" links, ask the webmaster/digital editor to remove the "nofollow" tag. There may be a terrible policy that they can't. Possibly remove them from your media list upon hearing this.

> » Politely remind the contact that "nofollow" links are intended to mark content as sponsored (paid) and unless you paid for the placement it is not the correct use of "nofollow."

- Competitive analysis. Check out your competitors with these tools to inventory where their links are coming from. Imitate the kind of coverage they've received. If they've gotten links from so and so, why couldn't you?

All of the services above are linked to on **PRtalk.co**, along with many PR Talk podcast episodes:

#28 with Carolyn Shelby while she was Director of SEO/ SEM for Tribune Publishing (which includes notable publications such as the Chicago Tribune and LA Times).

#31 with Greg Retsinas while he was the Director of Digital for KGW Media Group and the Regional Director for TEGNA.

#101 with Rand Fishkin, CEO of SparkToro and founder (former CEO) of Moz.

SOCIAL PR: TARGETING PRESS THROUGH SOCIAL MEDIA

It's hard to really go into depth on something that is destined to change. PR and the basic principles of doing it the right way will likely never change. However, the way in which we execute our discipline could.

I'm so old that I used to send press releases via fax. And then we'd have to call to follow up on them. Every single one. We couldn't wait for an email notification that the release was received.

When email came around it probably changed many industries. The same *could* be true for social media in some industries. As far as social media relates to PR, it is currently a way of amplifying our already solid PR efforts. I don't know that I would even call it a PR tool. It's just another way of getting in front of the press.

Here are the ways we can use social media to amplify, not replace, our PR efforts:

Connecting With Press On Social Media

Sure. If press is unresponsive to your emails, or you're having a hard time tracking email addresses down, ping them through social. They may be more responsive or appreciate you going through the extra effort. However, from my experience, even the hippest of Millennial press use their email inbox for work. That means the important work things, such as pitches and press releases, need to land inside inboxes, which essentially serve as filing systems for upcoming or ongoing work. You may be able to get their attention through social but I'm assuming that if it works, they'll ask you to email them.

Research Through Social Media

Using social to stay on top of what's happening in the media and with your contacts is the game changer. Twitter is great for this because you can follow anyone. Through a social media management platform, like Buffer or Hootsuite, arrange your targets in columns based on what they are covering to segment out all of your research. As we know, active research in PR is paramount.

On the surface, research enables you to connect with the media in a more meaningful way. Research allows you to complement media stories with follow up ideas, find new sources and discover different angles. However, on a deeper level, research helps you tune in to the craft of the news and understand what journalists are focusing on. Staying on top of current events and trends allows you to work from an instinctual level rather than going through the motions — the hallmark of an expert.

Beef Up Your Online Connections

Why not? It really does serve as a way to get to know your media contacts on a more intimate level. However, it's important that you recognize what each social medium is for and do not overstep your boundaries.

A PEEK INTO SOME SOCIAL MEDIUMS

LinkedIn

LinkedIn is like your online rolodex. I connect with everyone on LinkedIn because I don't like to keep business cards. In a perfect world, I would connect with every person I have a business dealing with through LinkedIn, whether I meet them in person at a networking event or I'm actively working with them. Ideally, I would also use this platform to connect with every single reporter who has ever written me back. However, no one is perfect.

Facebook

You likely know Facebook started as the place where friends meet online. While it is ever-changing as more and more businesses post on it, you probably wouldn't try to connect with press here unless you're friendly with them. This doesn't necessarily have to mean that you've met in person, you could be emailing or speaking frequently and have a lot in common, such as being around the same age, both raising kids or embarking on the same hobbies. The exception to the rule is if they're trying to build an online following. In that case, friend them and they will hardly notice, but you will look good by adding them to your online profile of connections and you could continue to deepen your understanding of who they are and what they're looking to cover.

Instagram

Think of Instagram as the place for images. More and more "friends" are moving over to this platform as Facebook is becoming a corporate or political stomping ground. Hey, Facebook isn't worried! They own Instagram! Here's where people who want to see pictures of Sally's newborn niece, Ryan's recent kitchen remodel, or Edwardo's fluffy puppy go. Even though it's a more casual platform than Facebook, I'd say the same rules apply for following press here because at the time of this writing, Instagram is just becoming a Facebook replacement.

Twitter

Twitter can seem like a free-for-all because you can "follow" anyone. A main goal for many Twitter personalities is to build a following. However, many of us, even press, use Twitter as voyeurs. To give you an idea of how the press uses it, TV stations' assignment desks used to rely on listening to the police scanners for their local news. Police scanners allow you to hear what the police are saying to each other, thus quite insightful for picking up breaking news. However, that all changed when Twitter came onto the scene. Now Twitter is used very much like police scanners were back in the day. Assignment editors have told me that Twitter breaks the news over police scanners today. The assignment desks' Twitter feeds are constantly running in the background, much like the police scanners.

What does this have to do with our role as PR professionals? You could be scanning key influencers, many of them press but not always, to shape your ideas. A portion of a PR department can be modeled like a newsroom, with Twitter feeds leading the charge.

So the long and short of it is: yes, follow anyone and everyone on Twitter so long as you aren't following anyone that could be too politically incorrect, since anyone can see who you are following. Use a social media platform to organize who you follow on Twitter into topics so you can compartmentalize, otherwise a shit-show of information will be flying at you.

Not sure where to get started? Try using Followerwonk to find journalists and other influencers on Twitter.

Pinterest

Cyberspace is filled with information, sparking millions of ideas. How does one organize it all? Enter Pinterest. This is where you can catalogue all of the ideas — from remodeling and decorating themes to recipes and party planning — not only in one place, but by category. A lifestyle brand can get an edge here if its online presence is maximized, allowing customers to catalog images and content into their Pinterest boards. PR needs to help social media teams with image as Pinterest can be used to further branding efforts.

SOCIAL ADVERTISING: STALKING REPORTERS THROUGH SOCIAL ADVERTISING

Let's step beyond Social Media 101 for a minute. If you're having a hard time getting coverage, explore the idea of targeting social media advertising toward your press targets. Turn your media pitch into a social post that ideally links to a press story or a more detailed blog post on your website. Then turn that social post into an advertisement that is directly targeted to press targets. It's a sneaky way of getting inside their heads — warming up a cold call — after you've diligently researched and created the perfect pitch.

Since **Facebook** offers more in-depth targeting options, here's how to advertise toward press targets within this platform:

- Create a custom audience (called a "Saved Audience" in Facebook)

- Specifically, target journalists (or anyone) based on advanced targeting. Narrow down by:

  » Geographic Area. For example, if you want to get a story in front of Portland Tech Journalists via Facebook start by using the location "Portland, Oregon." You can narrow down the geographic area to smaller than a zip code or wider than a city.

  » "Detailed Targeting." Include or exclude people with things like job title, interests, employers, education, etc. Mock-up a persona of your target and include/exclude based on that.

If this sounds too easy, it might be. Not everyone enters their employment information, so Facebook also uses their algorithm to guess occupations. But you can target specific "behaviors" and "interests" that would infer job titles. While you could target places of employment, you don't necessarily want to target advertising reps at any employer.

Also, depending on how specific your target audience is, you may have to expand beyond it because Facebook requires a minimum size of 20 people within the potential audience.

Targeted Advertising on Platforms Besides Facebook

Instagram: Since this platform is owned by Facebook, you can use the Facebook ad platform to target and display ads the same way in Instagram.

LinkedIn: This platform offers similar, but not as advanced, targeting as Facebook. While there is more information about titles and where people work, LinkedIn tends to be more expensive than Facebook.

Twitter: You can also advertise Tweets using demographics like Facebook.

AMPLIFYING PR RESULTS
WITH SOCIAL MEDIA

Once you do land that coveted story, continue maximizing its impact by leveraging it through social media. Press coverage is a wonderful way to say, "hey, I'm great," without having to actually say "hey, I'm great." That's because the press is doing the heavy lifting for you. Even if they didn't actually say "hey, this guy is great," they may as well have said that by simply including you in the story.

Don't worry too much about what was said in the article because many people don't actually read articles shared on social media. Nevertheless, sharing an article that simply mentions you highlights the fact that you're getting press attention. You can maintain your sense of class by not taking a braggadocious approach to saying that *Such and Such Magazine* wrote about you. All that's needed instead is a simple thank you (with tag!) to *Such and Such Magazine* for including you as a reference in the story. By doing this, your audience will see that you were included in *Such and Such Magazine*. It's likely they won't actually open the link and scroll down to realize that you were buried on page three. And if they do, at least you were included over your competitors.

SOCIAL MEDIA'S
INFLUENCE OVER NEWS

For the most part, stories are still released via traditional news outlets, including websites and blogs. However, since the early 2000s to 2021 today, social media is playing a large role in influencing the impact of that news. The more a story is shared, and who shares it, directly impacts the consumption of that news, reaching a greater and more diverse audience with shares from reporters or other influencers.

Many media outlets currently employ social media professionals on the editorial side. These social media professionals aren't necessarily breaking news. Rather, they work toward getting more eyeballs on their outlet's news through social media. While they could write social media copy, many of them aren't actually writing news, but restructuring copy that's already been written as news. They also may be in charge of how the media organization's website displays the news filed by their reporters.

In the fierce fight for eyeballs, the media outlet with the best social media department likely wins.

CONTENT MARKETING: REPURPOSING PR WORK

Any copy, or content, you write as a PR professional can be transformed into a different piece with the right augmentation. For instance, a press release can turn into a blog post, a white paper can turn into a bylined article, and a media pitch can be transformed into a social post.

Unfortunately too many teams are siloed and unable to take advantage of what they can do together. While many content teams create content calendars to plan, organize and assign online marketing functions like blog posts and social media posts, many other teams operate independently without sharing "the goods" between teams.

Overarching Marketing Calendars

Be the savvy, helpful PR professional that I know you are and expand your content team's calendar into an overarching editorial calendar that includes PR campaigns and more from the communications team.

And if one day you find yourself tasked with drafting your first content/editorial calendar, know that it can take its cues from the PR timeline. The topics found within many a PR timeline can bring logical, if not interesting, structure to other plans.

Content/editorial calendars can be built around the hard news (stuff you know is happening, such as the launch of a new product) already outlined in the PR timeline. They can also find inspiration from the

PR timeline's more casual aspects, such as remembrance days. Pitches or press releases inspired by such ideas could be customized by the content team for blog or social posts.

All of this could be viewed from the other way, with the content team informing PR's calendar. It really shouldn't matter, especially to a streamlined team, which team's plan helps build out the other team's calendar.

Sharing PR Results

You can share the media coverage you've garnered on social media a little bit differently through linking to the coverage on your website by blogging about it there, instead of sharing coverage that links back to a media website. That way your own website (otherwise known as "owned media" because you own and fully control that website) is being promoted in the social sphere.

The blog post doesn't have to be long. Just a couple of paragraphs will do; describing how the piece was put together, acknowledging and thanking the reporter/media outlet, and possibly delving into aspects the reporter didn't cover.

Beyond blogging about coverage, at some point a press room could be created for everything PR-related, such as: press releases/fact sheets, press coverage, photo galleries, contacts and more.

AWARDS STRATEGY: THE GAME OF WINNING HARDWARE

You know those braggers who boast about being awarded "Fastest Growing Something" or the "Healthiest Workplace?" I ate kale today, does that count? Well, jealousy is the sincerest form of flattery, so you may also want to consider putting together a strategy to identify and seek public-facing awards. Most of these awards are given by print or online news media. So for the most part, PR people are the ones behind securing them, and also promoting any wins that might arise through social media or other PR channels.

Why Spend the Time?

Examine your goals to determine if they align with what winning an award might do. Your answers will dictate the types of awards you'll go after. However, unexpected consequences can arise from award wins. For example, you may think that winning an industry award will only bring visibility among peers and competitors, which isn't what you're after. However, industry credibility can armor you against future disasters or accomplish future goals, such as recruiting new talent.

A self-indulgent, albeit very important, reason to get after awards is job security — whether you are in-house or agency-employed, or the client or service provider. When Veracity was applying for the Spectrum Marketing Awards, organized by the Northwest Credit Union Association, I distinctly remember how invested our credit union client was in providing us the details we needed to submit, and ultimately win, the award. The win proved to his boss that he was managing their PR firm well and we were worth the investment.

It should go without saying, but the additional marketing perks that award wins bring are undeniable, including: blogging topics, social content and hopefully, quality links back to your website.

Weeding Down the List

Ok, but still, where do you start? Examining who you are and what you do can help you start somewhere. Identify what types of awards you'd qualify for in the first place. Are you a large startup or a small family business? Minority or publically-owned? What industry are you in? Or what industry do you help? If you work at an agency, you can enter the client work you've done within award categories relating to their industries.

There are also many types of awards, including: numbers-based performance and size categories, employee surveys (best company to work for, healthiest workforce), geographic location, industry-related work, campaign-based work (for marketing awards), philanthropic (biggest donor/top volunteer) and more.

If you are even more overwhelmed now, here are some ways to pare down the list:

- **Qualification Conundrums.** First and foremost, simply qualifying might help take care of the problem. Your numbers, size, sales figures or industry might prohibit you from qualifying for some awards.

- **Budget Constraints.** Some awards require an entry fee. If you don't have a budget for that, you can weed out all fee-related opportunities. But maybe you can stomach a small registration fee from a nonprofit or trade group.

- **Geographic Location.** If you are based in Minnesota and only sell your product in Minnesota, well then, why would you submit your company for an award that will only be seen by an audience in Florida? (Yes, obviously I know it would be for the website link, but that is not the point here!)

Finding Awards

Once you've set your parameters and have an understanding of what's realistic, you'll have to plan ahead and determine which awards you'll target. There are four ways to do this:

1. Stalk your industry associations or your clients' industry associations. They probably offer some types of awards. If they aren't readily apparent on the association's website, look at the annual conference since the awards are typically bestowed to award recipients there.

2. Review local award opportunities. In Portland, that would be with *The Oregonian*, *Portland Business Journal* and *Oregon Business* magazine, among others. It also depends on industry, for example local awards through *Eater* would apply to those in the food/hospitality industry.

Since the same award typically only runs once a year, you may not be able to find them within your targeted outlets. Review the editorial calendars for a closer look. Once you get your feet wet with local opportunities, then possibly branch out to more mainstream opportunities like *Inc.*, provided you are large enough.

3. The database AwardZee might also help you. While I don't think it's regularly updated, the awards recycle year-after-year so the previous year's list is probably still pretty accurate.

4. And of course, Google can be an award-seeker's best friend.

How to Win

The good news is that once you've completed all of the above, you've drastically brought your winning chances up from zero to way, way higher. The hardest part is knowing about the award and staying organized enough to submit for it (we use Google Sheets to organize). Just put the dang deadline in the calendar so you don't let the opportunity pass you by. After that, here are some other things to consider:

- **Get an important person to nominate you/your organization(s).** I know your mom is your biggest supporter but when a nomination form must be filled out by a person your chances increase when your nomination comes from a notable contact.

- **Fill out the form for your contacts.** Don't expect a busy influencer to have the time, nor your messaging, to properly fill out the nomination form. Complete the nomination form, and then run it by them, before submitting anything under their name.

- **Honesty is the best policy.** Of course, when you're filling out the form be honest. There is no point in winning an award that you haven't actually earned only to be discovered later as a fraud.

- **Remember to try, try, and try again.** If you don't win, that doesn't mean you couldn't go after it again the following year. You'll have more time under your belt to qualify for success.

Marketing Award Wins

Your hard work doesn't stop after you've won. Now you need to tell the world! How you choose to do that might need to match how humble or braggadocious your organization's voice already is. But, if you don't maximize the award win, what was the point of going after it in the first place? Here are some high-level marketing tips to implement after winning:

- **Show up.** If there is an awards ceremony, show up to accept your award. Not only is it gracious, you can use the pictures for additional marketing on social media, PR or on your website.

- **Share on social media.** More than once. You could announce your win after finding out, and then later share photos of the awards event.

- **Blog about it.** The submission process or the work you did that garnered the award could be good blog fodder. Share the blog post a few times on social!

- **Share with staff and partners.** Make it easy for your staff or partners to share with their networks. They may want to show off what their company is accomplishing. This is true for all good PR.

- **PR it?** You could possibly announce big national awards to community or industry press. However, many outlets don't write about award wins. Also, *Forbes* is not going to care that you made the top whatever list in Nashville. There is also the competition factor. If the award was given by a media outlet, a different media outlet won't want to write about it.

- **Sales & Marketing Collateral.** Your sales staff can use the award to follow up with prospects, announce it in your email newsletter, and if there is a logo or badge indicating you are an award-winner, please add that logo to your website!

General Caveats

Once you get in your groove, winning awards left and right, it can be tempting to go after every award that presents itself. The only problem with doing so is that you must think about the nominators. If you're relying on your staff to take surveys about how great of an employer you are, after a while they'll start thinking you're not so great and indicate so either in the survey or in their work performance. A client of ours calls this "survey fatigue." You also don't want to keep asking the same contacts for their help in nominating you for an award. Be thoughtful about who you continue to approach and possibly don't say yes to every party you're invited to.

Good luck and may the awards force be with you!

ADVERTISING: WHO DOES THIS ANYMORE?

After getting through most of this book you are beginning to understand the power of PR and are likely wondering why anyone would advertise anymore, but it would take a hermit not to see the prolific ways in which companies are trying to get inside our psyche through advertising. From the flashy billboard that screams down at you to the more subtle newspaper ad that softly beckons you — advertisements are everywhere.

The most common forms of advertising that my firm works with are social advertising (beyond the way previously outlined to hold influence over the news) and online advertising — whether on websites through banner advertising or in search engines through pay-per-click. We find that most of our clients serve the behind-the-screen type of customer, within either the B2B or consumer markets. The vast ways in which we can reach audiences online hold amazing tracking capabilities that truly drive home the point of advertising to both ourselves and the client through bottom-line results.

At Veracity, for any type of advertising where we aren't just trying to drive home a branding message, like in a quick drive-by billboard, we find that taking a true PR approach is most effective for audiences. To us, a true PR approach leads with knowledge, information and empowerment, ahead of the "sell," in everything that we do, including advertising. The "sell," or ask, is then a result of knowledge-based messaging and better received.

For instance, now you know that you'd never distribute a press release that reads like an advertisement. It's got to have some substance, some news to it. Then the client message, or the "sell" is a side-note that becomes an inherent piece of the resulting coverage, but in a more sneaky, brain-washy type of way.

But, wait a sec, look at what I've just done. I've just now given advertising a bad rap by using the standard line most old PR hacks use: "a press release shouldn't read like an advertisement." Well if advertisements are all that negative, why should an advertisement read like an advertisement?

Advertisements with knowledge-based messaging help inform the audience, whether that information is about how to do something, tips that entertain, or valuable insight into key things that might help people make better decisions (such as through stats, trends and predictions).

I realize that it sounds like I'm advising you to create an advertisement that reads like a long blog post or a video and you're wondering how you'd make that visually appealing within a small design space. The small ad simply drives people to the long-form messaging. The call-to-action (CTA) within the ad directs audiences to the longer form messaging, but on the way you may have additional asks that meet your goals, such as requiring email addresses to access the helpful, long-form messaging.

By combining knowledge-based messaging with moment-in-time advertising, you're also combining multiple marketing disciplines. By doing it this way, multiple teams — such as the long-form copy, design and media-buying teams — open lines of communication for additional brainstorming and maximization of what's already in process. For example, practiced PR people do not overlook the media-buying team since an advertising budget could be leveraged, and even negotiated, through earned media.

I'll just end this section by saying that we do not claim to be advertising experts. I am only telling you a little of what I have experienced, because there are advantages to be gained when PR and advertising can collaborate.

CHAPTER ELEVEN

TYING IT ALL TOGETHER

You might say this book is backwards.

The logical place to start most things is with a clear plan of action that elevates a solid strategy. But, as have I mentioned, you must start somewhere.

At its core, this book is a training manual. When you go into any new field, you aren't tasked with doing the most important item first. You are given small jobs to increase your understanding and competence to then build up to the more strategic and advanced tasks.

Think of approaching PR in the same way. PR can be intimidating for even the most seasoned of workers in other industries. Therefore, the best place to start is with a warm-up that can bring actual results, confidence, and insights for the upcoming plan.

Moreover, the simple act of *doing* a little PR before getting overwhelmed and stalled by the planning stage can bring insights that will shape-shift your plan and bring efficiency to the process.

At our best, PR people are shape-shifters. Changing our approach for each client, press contact and scenario. That means our PR plans are never finalized. My clients and colleagues know that our plans always live in draft form because priorities or current news may change, completely upending previous plans.

Simply starting with the act of *doing*, and then changing course as you go, sometimes remembering to bring your newly gleaned insight back to the plan, sometimes scrapping the plan altogether — while never scrapping the activities of the PR for the cause, client or organization — is how to live the maximized PR lifestyle.

BUILDING YOUR PR PLAN

A PR plan starts with identifying goals, selecting audiences and determining how to make waves within each audience group (strategy) before finally moving on to outlining the roadmap for how you will complete it all (messaging and tactics). Since this is a book about *doing,* 99 percent of it focuses on tactics. Instead, here I'll give you a brief look at strategy.

Identifying Goals

Start by examining the overall goals of the organization and work from there. Outline how you can help the organization reach its goals. Keep in mind, every organization has its own set of unique goals that may surprise you; *not all are about making money.*

It's always a good idea to involve key stakeholders (company founders, nonprofit board members, long term customers) to ensure you've got a strong handle on the goals. When it's time to set out how the PR goals can propel the organizational goals, you'll have some allies and hopefully be on the same page.

This research can be done in a multitude of ways:

- Interviews, I find verbal to be the best, but written email Q&A's can work in a pinch.

- Reading past documents about the organization's history or key milestones.

- Good old conversations, whenever they present themselves, are always the best.

Once you have a handle on the organizational goals, uncover how PR can help back those goals. Here are some common organizational ambitions, *besides sales and increased revenue*, with their PR goal sidekicks:

- Attracting and retaining talent — PR works to communicate a positive workforce and working environment, leading to a goal of attracting and retaining employees through PR.

- Helping others through a nonprofit's mission — PR works to elevate the nonprofit's cause, leading to a PR goal of increased public knowledge about the cause, solidifying its importance among audiences to drive involvement, donations and support.

- Helping others through a business service — PR works to elevate the need for the service, solidifying its importance among audiences to drive awareness and ultimately sales.

- Helping others through technology or products — PR works to elevate the need for the product, solidifying its importance among audiences to drive awareness and ultimately sales.

Secondary goals that the PR goals listed above can help drive:

- Increasing profits for employees and owners through increased revenue, creating opportunities for raises/profit sharing/bonuses.

- Increasing profits for the shareholders, ultimately affecting employees.

- Increasing funding through donations/government grants, ultimately affecting nonprofit services provided.

MAPPING STRATEGY THROUGH TACTICS

I've written my share of PR plans — that have evolved into marketing plans — for clients over the last 20 years. If I start with the PR strategy, I find that tactics fall into place. Create a year-long plan through mapping out what will be done each month for 12 months. The 12-month PR timeline can also morph into other marketing disciplines.

Creating Your PR Timeline

Depending on your preferred style, do not operate in a linear fashion when scheduling your first PR plans month-by-month. Your first instinct may be to focus on the upcoming month and then move forward to the next month. It can work, but it can also create writer's block. It may be better to first list the 12 months you need to schedule, and then place the following details in each month, not in order of months:

- Upcoming events or major activities that your organization is planning or hosting and major sales promotions or milestones. Does your organization have an anniversary coming up?

  » In the timeline, also include when to start working on the PR to get it released and placed in time, which differs from when the event/promotion/milestone actually takes place.

- Upcoming events (such as tradeshows or conferences) your organization will be attending, sponsoring (even better!) or speaking at (better yet!).

» In the timeline, also include when to start working on the PR to get it released and placed in time, which differs from when the events actually take place.

- Editorial calendar opportunities for which you plan to submit PR pitches. You'll want to include the appropriate lead times in your calendar to allow for ample time to submit your pitch. You might even want to have the Ed Cal topic listed in the month it's set to run (even if you don't make it in) because it gives you a pulse on what the press is covering, allowing you to leverage other short-lead press opportunities. The Ed Cal topics may even provide good social media fodder because they tend to trend toward what people are thinking about at the time.

  » Your Ed Cal pitches can expand into blog and social media posts to reach more people.

- Appropriate seasonal or holiday themes, such as Valentine's Day for a chocolate company and "School's Out for Summer" for a theme park.

  » What press releases, blog posts and social media posts can you create around these themes?

- National awareness days and months, ranging from the more serious like National Water Safety Month to the sillier such as National Chip & Dip Day (a desperate PR person may have created this but I don't even know if it exists).

  » You can easily tie press releases/pitches and blog/social posts into timely angles like these.

  » I've listed many ways to find these on PRtalk.co.

- Additional news that you know will come out of your organization, such as the launch of a new product or service or the opening of a new location. While the planned timeframes may shift, you at least have an idea, so get it down on paper to start thinking ahead.

- Public awards that apply to your organization or its executives.

And, wallah! After doing all of the above you'll find that your PR timeline is pretty much done. If you have a few months that aren't filled in, that is okay. Trust me, if you are actively working on your PR you will add more as time goes on. Or, you can reserve the blank spaces to accomplish tasks you've been putting off, such as creating a crisis response plan. Also you'll be shifting things around constantly to mirror changing priorities and emerging developments. The PR timeline is always in "draft" mode and never "set." Everyone on my team knows this, especially the client. As such, it leaves room for creativity and initiative.

SELECTING AUDIENCES

When thinking about PR goals, I always imagine the people who'd consume the news stories we might dream up — audiences. PR professionals can get tripped up in this section, thinking that the media is our only audience. That isn't true. We use the media as a means to get to our ultimate audience — whether they be consumers, business people (who are also a type of consumer, but just in a different capacity), employees/other stakeholders, politicians/policy makers, analysts and other types of decision makers.

To discover your audience, examine your goals and the audience should fall into place. You'll likely have more than one audience, so tier them based on their level of importance in order to structure how much effort each audience deserves because they aren't all equal. After identifying and segmenting your audience, you'll ferret the media audiences from there.

Understanding Audiences
After deciding *who* you will reach, the question about *how* you will

reach your audience remains. You must uncover what they care about, what messages will stick and what they're consuming. There are many fancy ways of digging into the minds of each conceivable target audience. Big firms pay big bucks for "focus groups" and psychological research. But they're the Campbell's soup and Nike-type level. Those of us working in mid-sized PR firms, at a startup, or for a nonprofit do not have the luxury of bottomless budgets nor time. We must act. Now. We mostly do that through instinct.

The older we are, the better because we can draw on past memories to put ourselves in the shoes of many audiences. Don't worry if you're young. The more empathetic you are, the easier it is to put yourself in a stranger's shoes. Try to project yourself into the future and imagine what it will be like when you retire. What do you think your priorities will be? How do you think you will feel about things? Or if you're old like me, imagine being the age of what we call the "millennials" again. After doing these kinds of exercises, think about who might provide further insight. If you have a millennial intern, their insight could be invaluable depending on the client. Or, call your retired parents and ask what they are reading, what do they care about?

I understand that while these sound like great exercises, you might be busy. The good news is that the target audience might be sitting right underneath your nose. If you're working for a firm, the client likely IS the target audience. Or on the organizational, or client side, your boss could closely mirror the audience. In many cases people somehow end up working for what they believe in. I don't mean to sound idealistic, but I've discovered this through experience. If they don't entirely represent the audience, they likely understand your audience better than most. Lean on them.

CHAPTER TWELVE

LIVING THE
PR LIFESTYLE

As we've worked through the mechanics of PR, know that we're just getting started. Multiple books can be written on more advanced levels of PR, including one for strategy, planning and research, along with another for crisis prevention and management, and yet another explaining all of PR's "step sisters" (related fields and industries).

I hope by now you are encouraged. You have a solid foundation with working knowledge of PR fundamentals. This most important insider-knowledge will carry you toward an exciting, ever-changing career in PR.

The next phase is getting your boots on the ground. As you get going, I hope you will become a PR pro who truly lives the PR lifestyle. The PR lifestyle shows you what works and what doesn't on a company-by-company, story-by-story, or contact-by-contact basis. With your confidence built, you'll rewrite the rulebook for each unique scenario. In fact, living the PR lifestyle means that in a world where news consumption and popular culture is constantly changing, it is my hope that you will be bold enough to forget all that is written in this book and forge your own path.

With that said, no matter where you are on your rule-following journey, there are a few characteristics that will always define those who live the PR lifestyle. In this last chapter, I'll leave you with the most important elements of the PR lifestyle principles. While I'll present them in a way that can be applied to your role as a PR professional, know that they can carry you toward success in any career.

Living the PR lifestyle means:

- Going deep through maximization
- Following good practices of reading and writing
- Partnering with other people
- Developing an "on-the-offense" crisis mindset
- Seeking to discover and evolve your story

THE MAXIMIZED STYLE

The difference between maximized PR and regular old mediocre PR is how deep you'll go into any single campaign. I guess you could consider this to be true in any job function. Maximizers are willing to uncover every angle, try a variety of tactics or reach out to different people in myriad ways. Maximizing your efforts is the precursor to how successful you will be.

I used to view this quite simply. The harder you work at PR'ing something, the better the results will be. Today I know it's not that simple. Now I believe PR success is about energy. No matter what type of work you're doing, the more concentrated brain space a project receives, the more positive the results will be.

The maximizing PR person takes their projects with them into the shower, into traffic jams, and into movie theaters. When we care about our craft, our work reserves precious headspace.

Maximizers don't do anything halfway and neither should you. People who are great at PR aren't just distributing a press release and calling it a day. They're delving into all angles of the campaign, such as:

- Paying attention to the news, letting either current events or the way in which specific journalists report affect their next moves.

- Shifting between PR materials (pitches, fact sheets, press releases) based on how they are being received.

- Changing pitches and outreach methodology for each reporter or outlet, based on previous relationships, the target's location or the target's focus area.

- Following up relentlessly. That doesn't mean hounding the same target, it means switching gears to hone in on different targets within the same outlet if you aren't having success, moving on to different outlets, or again, changing your angle until it works.

You might be confused here, recalling the press etiquette standards outlined in Chapter 4. However, there are appropriate ways around the standards, enabling you to follow the rules *and* get after it. Always abide by the press etiquette rules, using Rule #6 as a general guide: **never follow up more than twice with the exact same pitch to the exact same contact.** After head-butting into Rule #6, do the following things to remain aggressive, yet tactful:

1. **Get a new contact** — maybe your idea is good enough, but you're pitching the wrong person.

2. **Change the angle of your idea** — by tweaking it according to current events or what the media is writing about.

3. **Start over** — create a whole new idea for the same project or client.

However, the idea of maximizing your PR shouldn't only surface when you're having trouble. PR isn't for the faint of heart, so if you're doing it right you'll have a lot of trouble, but hopefully you'll hardly notice. Constantly repeating numbers 1 and 2 in the list above separates you from mediocrity.

Remember you can view the maximized style of working from the lens of success. There are things you can do to amplify the success you are having. An example of amplifying an already fine campaign is through location-based marketing. It's a process that can turn what may have only been one story into 20 different stories — if you're diligent enough to make it happen.

LOCATION. LOCATION. LOCATION.

That famous phrase is most often connected to real estate, but it should also be aligned with PR. Any time you can sneak ANY type of local angle into your story, do it! Not only does a local angle mean an extra story for your PR report, a local story online might even be better than a nationally-focused story for your SEO or overall marketing goals.

There are many ways to insert a local angle through leading with the location where your news is occurring. Here's what I mean:

- **Headquarter location:** Anything a business or charity does is likely to be news to the outlets based in the community where their headquarters are located, assuming the area is small enough. If you are headquartered in a large urban metropolis, this might not be applicable. But more and more organizations are selecting office locations in surrounding suburbs of larger cities — many of them also being home to smaller community media.

- **Office location:** Assuming your business or charity has multiple office locations, tweak the lead in the press materials and email subject line to convey the appropriate geography for each office — only if there is an outlet specifically covering that area — even if the news comes out of the headquarter office.

For example, your company, headquartered in Austin, Tx., wins a noteworthy award. You also happen to have four additional office locations, each with their own community paper covering that specific town. So you can't say the satellite office, located in Burbsville, got the award because it was a company-wide effort. But in the first sentence of the press release and/or pitch you can say: "Cool Guy Company, *which has an office located in Burbsville*, received the Most Hipster Millennials in Tech Award." Then you'll go on to explain somewhere that the company is headquartered in Austin.

- **Service areas:** For any charity or business serving a distinct set of areas. Follow the above format, but make your service area clear. If you have reasons to serve that geographical area specifically, consider including the reason you serve each area in your press communications.

- **Staff / key stakeholder current resident area, hometown or college town:** If the news relates to something a specific person is doing, such as joining a board, recently being hired or promoted, etc., absolutely dig into this person's location background and add the local connection to the communications.

Remember, if you are ever pitching a locally-focused community outlet, the only way it will work is if you tout the local angle front-and-center because they only cover what's affecting their local community. Make sure to include the specific location information both in the email subject line and high up in the email message or press release. They are used to getting unrelated items, so make sure they don't have to search for the location information, otherwise it will end up in the trash.

BECOMING A WRITER

Being a fluent writer will help you get through many tough situations with more efficiency and ease, while also helping you tell stories either more accurately or with a higher level of skill, enabling you to land coveted earned media placements.

However, there is a journey toward becoming a writer. You aren't just born with the skill. It's like anything else that takes practice and diligence, just like the entire field of PR. In the case of becoming a writer, the most important thing you can do is frequently read. The second most important thing you can do is write a lot, which really shouldn't be a problem in this industry!

Read to Learn How to Write

"The best way to sharpen your writing skills is to read," Jim said. Remember my first boss? Of the many tips he gave me, this was the first time I'd heard this particular tip but it wouldn't be the last. All of the great writers point to this tip. To paraphrase Stephen King's thoughts about this from his writing memoir, "On Writing," those who do not like reading have no business trying to write, because writing begins with reading.

Actually "On Writing" was the precursor to me writing this book. However, my story as a writer begins much before that. It started with the worried perfectionist, checking over her shoulder at every turn on the keyboard. The very first time I set down the words "For Immediate Release," I experienced that slight feeling of stomach butterflies. But looking back I think that indicated how much I cared about the job of PR, rather than a sign of my insecurities.

While Jim pointed to fiction, I found that reading press releases and past news articles helped as well. At night I began a diligent book reading practice that I am now more dedicated to than ever. Literature holds a place among the most important things in my life. Today, I can't sleep without reading from any old book. But during the day, I find that the more news articles I read, the easier it is to shape my press releases like them, which is the hallmark of a well-written press release.

Listening to news stories on TV and radio helps as well. Understanding how your pitch might sound on-air helps sneak PR messaging into the news hook with better finesse. The more we write like the news, the better the chances of it getting picked up without too much augmentation by the whim of newsrooms.

Write to Learn How to Write

I digress. Back to my personal story of becoming a writer. Beyond reading a lot, I found that simply writing a lot does wonders as well. This makes sense, though, right? You'll get better at anything with practice. But, the practice I am talking about might look different than what you're imagining.

The game changer for me was taking a free class through the nonprofit organization "Write Around Portland." During the class, a wonderful volunteer gave us prompts with a set time to respond through writing. We would then read our responses aloud. It was magical. And get this, it was all done on paper with pen. No computers or devices were allowed in the class. The prompts she gave us, the space she held for the pain some of us worked through, and the act of putting real pen to paper was therapeutic in a way I cannot describe. Showing up each week, I wrote with a frenetic abandon that changed the way I write forever.

Today I attack the page, get it all out, throw up on the page, no matter what I am writing. And then deal with the edits later. I can't tell you how much more effective, faster and freeing this approach is. The real work of the writer is actually setting down words on the page. Sure, I agree with many of the greats who say that the magic happens in the edits. However, the first thoughts that make it onto that blank white page, daring you to press on, are miracles.

Listen to Learn How to Write

As you press on, be receptive and thankful for many edits to your work. I learned the most about editing and writing from my work being completely ripped apart. Beyond reading the greats, the head writer at my second PR firm job, Deb, taught me the most about writing, through her edits.

It was when we still used pen and paper to mark changes on pages we'd actually print out, rather than use the "track-changes" tool in Microsoft® Word. She patiently took the time to explain every edit to me when sometimes it would have been easier for her to take over and completely rewrite the whole thing. There is something to hearing about why to make a change and then inputting the change yourself that helps commit the discipline to memory, rather than blindly accept them through "track-changes."

If you have found someone that will do this type of editing with you, know that they are an important sage that will impact the rest of your career, especially in this day and age when everyone is so focused on getting everything done quickly. Be very appreciative of this mentor and thankful for every single annoying edit, because with the right attitude, this extra work will up-level your game for life.

WORKING WITH OTHERS

You'll never really learn the basics in this book until you practice them in real life. Being good at PR is just like anything else you've ever tried to be good at before. Constantly using the PR muscle will strengthen your practice until you begin to flow effortlessly from situation-to-situation, client-to-client, problem-to-problem. Working from that instinctual place deep within will allow you to find success in any scenario, even if it means declining an opportunity in the name of a better long-term solution.

Partnering With PR Professionals: "PR-to-PR"

As your instinct strengthens, it doesn't mean you are working rouge, unless you absolutely have to. Practiced PR professionals still consult with colleagues, especially to confirm our original hunches. We find that collaborating with PR professionals is the highest form of PR. I call this "PR-to-PR."

Getting your message out among other PR professionals can be the best way to "PR something" because other PR professionals also have contacts and ideas. For example, if you have a client exhibiting at a tradeshow, your first contact should be the tradeshow's PR representative. Often partnering with them, beyond telling them what type of PR you are looking to generate through the tradeshow, can bring you additional goodies, such as the list of press attending the show, otherwise known as the "press list." And, if you outline how your client can benefit the show's PR — sometimes by simply being a ready, willing and *responsible* participant — you can piggyback on each other's efforts. We all work best together.

The Customer is Always Right

Don't let your budding confidence overshadow your better judgment and client relations. There's a lot of truth to the saying "the customer is always right." Oftentimes, if I bring a media problem to a client, typically if they are at the higher level, such as ownership or in the C-suite, they will know how to handle the situation. You will bring the problem to them, discuss options and quite possibly come up with a solution together. Or your client will instinctively know what to do, either regarding a small, but important, portion of the problem or the entire problem.

Remember that your client or boss has also been building their own type of professional muscle, probably holding more practice than you. They also have more at stake if they are on the client side, especially in the ownership realm, and there may be reasons they cannot go into with you, if they do not want to pursue an opportunity you have brought to them.

Of course there is a fine-line between being a pushover and being accommodating. The more you work in not just PR but also with a particular client or company, you will know when to fight for what you think is right. Remember to pick your battles and that humility is the best form of leadership, no matter who you are working with — the client, your team or the media — or how many years of experience you have.

CRISIS PREVENTION

Your ears, or eyes rather, may have perked up when you read the word "problem" in the previous section. Problems abound in PR and they range from the approachable type, like a story won't run, to the brain-bending type, such as a crisis. I haven't mentioned problems of the bigger variety because, again, this is an introductory book. But as time marches on, you'll find that PR is filled with problems big and small.

The small problems come in the form of building such great relationships, or such a good reputation for your client, that the press wants to include you in many stories that your client may not want to be included in. Either because they are controversial or the client is just not prepared to go down that road for whatever reason. After a while I have seen that my job as a PR person is to protect my clients' time, along with their reputation of course.

However, I don't often have to worry about my clients' reputations because I elect to work with ethical companies. This has everything to do with the organization's inside operations — from how employees are treated and hired to how the books are kept.

Don't have any problems to begin with and then you won't have any problems to deal with: The hallmark of crisis prevention.

And yet, crises happen to the most straight-laced, thoughtful and but-toned-down of them all. How you deal with the aftermath has a huge effect on how the outside world perceives the crisis.

Playing Offense

Crisis prevention puts you ahead of any crisis because nothing is unforeseen. If you think like Negative Nelly, you're closer to beating the crisis. Having an approved plan in place that outlines everyone's role, not only in general, but in the case of specific scenarios, eliminates the dangerous stalling time that can make or break how you're viewed in the event of a crisis. Remember, time is not on your side in the crisis. How swiftly, yet cleanly, you respond is of paramount importance. And responding "no comment" is never an option!

Using a crystal ball, sit down with your leadership team, and possibly legal counsel, to brainstorm the negative that could occur and how each situation should be handled to begin your crisis prevention plan. Then you will have a starting point to include these key elements in your plan:

- List possible crises that could occur.

- Outline designated spokespeople for each crisis, and in general.

- Create customized talking points for each possible scenario, along with company-standard talking points (if you don't already have them).

- Draft possible executive responses corresponding to each possible scenario. What you release could change depending on how the issue actually plays out, but at least you will have an approved starting point.

- You probably do not need to issue a full press release during the heat of a crisis, with the executive responses being more straight-forward and easier to change in the moment, nevertheless you could put some templates together if that makes the *you-sitting-in-the-front-row* feel better.

- Outline a plan of attack regarding how the materials will be disseminated to the press and how aggressive your team will be with proactive outreach depending on the problem.

- Outline guidelines for responding to press inquiries, in terms of designated response time and communication method, i.e. if the press *calls* you about a crisis, CALL (not text or email) them back ASAP, or within two hours.

Playing Defense

Even if you have a crisis plan in place, and especially if you don't, when the crisis hits you might lose all rational thought because you'll be in the heat of the heart-palpitating moment. So having any portion of the plan ready, no matter how rough, can do wonders for you in moments when you'd otherwise lose your head. Nevertheless, there are some key points to remember when dealing with a crisis from the PR side.

"No Comment" is not acceptable. Everyone knows there are two sides to every story. Believe it or not, we still live in a forgiving, and forgetful, society. Guide your executives in telling the organization's side of the story, no matter how shameful it might be.

Time is of the essence. Act swiftly. Do not take much time in pondering your responses (see below about taking time to call in an expert). If you take too long, you are giving the press leeway to run in the wrong direction with the story and you will further lose control of the situation. Your response doesn't have to sound like Shakespeare. It simply has to be clear, concise and above all, accurate.

Always tell the truth. No matter how bad the situation is. You must hold your executives accountable. You must serve as an investigator so you can get to the heart of what really happened and present your side of the story most accurately. You don't have to expand upon all of the details, but if you shade the truth, you're only digging a deeper hole. You might be buying more time, but when you're found out, because untruths are always uncovered, your crisis becomes that much bigger.

Remember other audiences. While your main concern might be traditional press, do not forget other audiences whether or not you are directly responsible for communicating with them and/or on the platforms where they are. As a PR person, your job should be advising all communication channels when a crisis hits. The customer, employee, shareholder/investor, and board of director audiences are sometimes even more important than the press audience. While the press audience ultimately reaches those audiences, those most important people, such as employees, could feel quite slighted if they glean crucial news from a third party. You must think about that in your crisis plan and disseminate press communications and internal communications either staggered or at the same time.

Call in an expert. If your crisis is truly of the very bad, or even shameful variety, by all means call in a true crisis or legal expert to help you! But do not let the vetting and waiting for their arrival stall you. There is no time in a crisis so you cannot interview multiple crisis responders and wait for them to finish the project they are on to start working on your project. If you've made it all the way to this portion of this book I know you are thoughtful enough to at least respond to some press inquiries on your own, if not get smack dab right in front of the crisis. I don't care if you are two years out of college. Put your big boy and girl pants on. Ask the tough questions. Then get your job done.

Ending the Game

Knowing when to walk away from a bad situation — such as a client, boss or company — is not just another form of living the PR lifestyle. It's a way of living a strong professional and personal lifestyle, no matter where your PR career takes you.

In a crisis, you need to get down to the heart of the matter through asking the hard questions. The top PR professional on a crisis case must know all the gritty details to serve their clients, the press and the public well. If you feel that the answers you are drawing out are insincere or frequently side-stepping the issue, listen to your instinct and walk away.

Maintain your ethical and personal integrity at all costs. If one day you become the owner of a PR firm like me, walk away if you have an off feeling, especially in the first moment of meeting with the troubled party. You do not need any proof. You may be losing money now but in the long-run you will gain integrity not only with yourself but also your colleagues, press and future bosses or clients. Or if you are employed, find a trusted colleague, with some seniority, that you can turn to for advice.

Losing a little money or opportunity now will save you in terms of time, worry and possibly embarrassment and heartache. Maintaining your professional reputation will likely result in your gaining more money down the road. Also if you aren't stewing on ethics you'll have more time to put toward something more productive and lucrative. Even if your professional reputation would not be on the line, but you have an "off" feeling or the job doesn't fit with your personal beliefs, respect yourself above all else and walk away.

You are always your most important client or boss and I believe in you, so please believe in yourself.

HOW MEDIA RELATIONSHIPS
WORK IN PR

Media relationships can be handy when you are in a crisis, by probably only just making you feel a little more comfortable, but in general I want to clear up some misconceptions I see about press relationships in PR. I am speaking from my experience and I really don't know what I don't know. But my thought is that relationships are not some big mystery in PR.

If you happen to be searching for a PR vendor one day and a candidate can only brag about the relationships they have, run the other way. If they are bragging about their relationships, one would wonder if they do any actual work.

Sure, relationships help us expedite our jobs. For example, the media contact list is already cleaned up and you might know what type of stories will work for specific contacts or media outlets. And in some cases you can make a friendly call to a reporter to shape a story to go a little more your way than it may have gone without that call.

Still, let's clear up the mystery around how those relationships are built. When PR people go around bragging about their relationships, they make the process sound really vague and hard. As if they are special people with some special "in" that you could never possibly gain without either working with them (from the potential client point-of-view) or being them (from the PR competitor point-of-view).

Most Media Don't Want to Socialize

Let me tell you a BIG secret that I want you to remember always. For the most part, media people, especially those working in print and online, are NOT social people. There aren't really any parties or happy hours where an anointed PR person holds court with the media. Occasionally you might find the rare social-butterfly or someone working at a cut-throat publication that relies on social connections and "scoops" (inside information). However, most of the media people I know would rather go home at the end of a long day and veg out.

If there are social opportunities happening, they are rare and on a case-by-case basis. For example, you may have mutual friends in common or are old friends from another era. I've mentioned my best childhood friend being a producer at many of the Portland area TV stations. In my younger days, we'd go out and party with some of her reporter colleagues, however I never really relied on those connections to get stories placed.

Build Relationships By Doing a Good Job

The reason I didn't resort to relying on those vague connections is because I knew how to do my job, and it wasn't by buying people drinks. If you follow the main PR principles, which roughly include pitching stories that are newsworthy and timely, along with doing research to send stories they'd actually cover, and also following press etiquette rules — which include being responsive, trustworthy and ethical — your relationships will be made.

To clarify, these are professional relationships that grow over time. They are not really that different from other professional relationships you'll make in the future, but sometimes they can become even stronger, not like in the doing-shots-at-closing-time variety, but in the colleague and partnership variety.

Also know that you can follow this model when attempting to pitch in a new location or new industry. If you just start out on the right foot, with an appropriate story that actually provides some value, you are entering the relationship immediately, with the first email. That's how PR firms are able to handle multiple clients all over the world and in many industries at once. Do you think they actually have relationships with thousands of reporters upon embarking into the new work that every new client demands? Impossible.

PROVING YOUR SALT

After all your work building relationships with media the true way — which actually results in coverage — the stories should be coming in. Capturing and reporting on the earned media you have generated is a big part of the PR job. You'll constantly vie for your position at the table or your place on the payroll.

Yet showing PR's worth has always been hard and top-of-mind during industry discussions. You can't always point to how much revenue results from a story, because most stories are general and not solely about one organization, therefore mostly boosting overall organizational branding and reputation. If a story does happen to focus solely on one organization, it still might not point to one specific call-to-action. Whereas a traditional advertisement can drive a specific outcome, such as purchasing one product, that can then be tracked with the sales pointing back to the value of the advertisement.

Enter the new world of online advertising, SEO and digital marketing. Proving our worth gets even harder when competing with these guys. In online advertising, especially pay-per-click (PPC), website clicks can be traced back to purchases or outcomes. Numbers-crunchers and decision makers typically feel more comfortable investing in quantifiable marketing and cannot wrap their heads around PR's difficulty to report in the same manner.

Expanding Our Reporting Horizons

PR people have to think beyond the press clipping report, with larger firms devoting entire divisions to this. It's no longer enough to just point to all the stories you've gained as proof of your effectiveness. The industry is trying all types of approaches.

If you can tie PR activities to conversions and/or key performance indicators (KPIs) — such as direct sales, leads, white paper downloads, video views and social engagement — you're closer to measuring your impact. An example of how you can do that is by inserting tracking or "vanity" links in your press releases and pitches. By tracking how many clicks the link receives when stories hit, and if that visitor took a desired action, you'll have a sense of impact. You'll probably have to work with teams outside of marketing, such as finance, analytics or IT, to get such information.

It goes back to understanding ultimate goals and discovering how PR can impact those goals — while measuring everything along the way.

Our Value is Bigger Than Outcomes

Even if you are getting strategic by measuring one-off outcomes like newsletter sign-ups, or even sales, it's still difficult to put a price on the value of PR, unless you work with the top executives in your quest to tie these one-off outcomes to larger organizational goals, like retention and recruiting, stakeholder engagement, or revenue. Regardless, what is the price of a positive brand? For some organizations, it could be priceless.

Some PR people attempt to attach the type of key metrics mentioned above to larger organizational goals through working with leadership as true partners. Some will even go so far as to tie their PR income to these results — like a traditional sales professional's payment, with a base plus commission. This sounds a little advanced and probably something you wouldn't try until later in your career or without the help of a mentor.

> For more on commission-based payments, listen to PR Talk podcast episode #89 with Ira Gostin on **PRtalk.co**

Frequent Reporting of Coverage

This doesn't mean that straight-up reporting of your coverage isn't important. Whenever a story lands, share it with your team, including your social team — possibly even with "suggested" social media text to run with the coverage, if budget allows.

Beyond that, you'll want to incorporate an in-depth reporting system that involves numbers — even if they don't point back to key metrics or revenue — that is sent to decision makers monthly, quarterly or yearly.

An in-depth report is literally a book of all the coverage. The important part is that it leads with a list of all the hits, like a table of contents, that includes the *advertising value* of each hit and the *publicity value*, ending with the numbers being totaled.

- **Advertising Value:** The cost of purchasing each piece of coverage as an advertisement. Someone will have to dig up the advertising values through each publication's media kit, which is cumbersome work, but well worth it.

- **Publicity Value:** Multiply each advertising value by the industry standard of 3 - 5 to add the credibility factor that PR brings. Remember that anyone can buy an ad, whereas it takes a very special company to be highlighted in the press for free, therefore the coverage is literally worth more than double of the advertisement cost.

We believe that all PR teams need to complete this practice at least yearly. It helps to consistently compile the coverage and update the advertising values within your media lists.

If you land a national news story, but the phone didn't ring, did you do a good job? Maybe you did because the organization can still use the coverage for credibility, sharing it on social and with key prospects. But if you aren't periodically pointing back to revenue being impacted, at some point the decision makers could forget about the national story and move in a different direction.

We attempt to ensure this doesn't happen through constant analysis. But, if an honest appraisal discovers traditional PR to be ineffective, living the PR lifestyle means that you are humble enough to let the PR work go, either offering the budget to a more effective marketing discipline, or switching gears, discovering new areas where your honed PR mindset can take you.

DISCOVERING YOUR STORY

And finally, your story. Do you see how after doing what's in this book you'll be closer to your story? In fact, this book will have you telling your story all along, bit-by-bit, with every pitch, press release and action.

By announcing what happens to you, or creating your own news, or commenting on the happenings of the world, your story will begin to unfold. It may not be perfect, but key opportunities won't be missed and you'll be getting it out there.

Just like a PR plan, your story is a living, breathing, changing thing that evolves over time. The beginning part is not so hard to tell because it's new — the launch of an organization, the birth of a company. It is the same after many years and much experience. The established organization has clout under its belt — real life has shaped its experience so that it and everyone else knows who it is.

It is this middle space between birth and old-age that is the most vague and difficult. This is where creativity, success and entire organizations go to die. But in the right setting, the talented PR person shines. When the story begins to lag, paling in comparison to the launch, the PR person brings new ideas, while supporting actions through announcing them to the world. With that, a new or continued story is shaped along the way.

Here themes begin to emerge underneath every action and decision:

For example, charitable donations and community involvement might begin to lean toward one category over another. This slant might align with the organizational mission or more accurately tell it. Such parameters around extracurriculars can sharpen mission and vision, directly impacting the story.

Or you could examine retention and recruitment. How and why staff choose to stay or join a company point to an organization's unique culture, further shaping the story once again.

Or the launch of new products and services can lean an organization into a new direction or further confirm its well-worn path, therefore solidifying a story that's already been told or taking it in a surprisingly new direction.

In all of these scenarios, the "story" is found within the why.

No one has a story if they don't get out there to make things happen, sitting in the shadows of their own life. So I challenge you now, get out there and discover yours!

ACKNOWLEDGEMENTS

Thank you to my first on-the-job guides: Jim Beriault, who's friendship taught me more than just the basics but also a love for the job. Monique Barton, who's example taught me the most in "maximization" with a flair. Debra Flickinger, my first writing sage who graciously explained all of her edits when it would have been easier to have written it herself.

Thank you to my long-term clients who served as mentors later in my career: Michael Weinhouse who is my client, brother and sounding-board in all things business and many things life. Joanie Allen, who will forever be my favorite client who is not related to me.

Thank you to my parents who stand by in awe as their children accomplish odd and unrelatable feats such as running a marathon, heading a national, multi-location company (not mine!) and writing a book during the coronavirus-schooling-children-and-running-a-business-from-home era. My father's consistency and diligent work ethic provided the perfect show-don't-tell example for us kids. My mother's creative business ventures provided inspiration into reinventing careers to fit lifestyles.

Thank you to my ultimate bosses in the order in which they have helped me on my most important journey: Erika Wrenn, Ciara Pressler, and Alyce Irving.

Thank you to my Ben and Audrey for serving as my initial inspiration towards my most important journey and the reason we have created a business (Veracity) that values life and love over profits. Ben, my heart melts every time you correct my assumptions. Audrey, your drive to do all the things all the time is impressive. We are rich in the time that we get to spend with you both.

And most importantly, *thank you to my partner in life*, parenting and business, Mike Rosenberg, my best friend, fiercest ally and the best husband a girl could ask for. Not only do you put up with my crazy ideas bombarding you at inconvenient times, but you actually believe in them and try to see them through (if only I would remain interested long enough!). To copy the phrase you so sweetly said in our wedding toast: "thank you for loving me."

ABOUT THE AUTHOR

Amy Rosenberg learned PR in the trenches — working her way up from intern to management at two marketing agencies before starting her own PR firm, Veracity, in 2008. As the firm's president, she oversees the blending of digital strategies with classic PR tactics to favorably position clients both online and in traditional media. Amy created her podcast, PR Talk, sponsored by the Public Relations Society of America (Oregon), in 2017 and has hosted more than 100 episodes so that PR people can better learn the craft. Amazingly, Amy is still married to the business partner (Mike Rosenberg) that joined her firm in 2011. They reside in Portland, Oregon with their two school-aged children (Ben and Audrey), dog (Rio) and cat (Roar).